Yes, You Can!

And Freeze and Dry It, Too

Published by Cool Springs Press
P. O. Box 2828, Brentwood, Tennessee 37024

Library of Congress Cataloging-in-Publication Data

Gasteiger, Daniel.
  Yes, you can! : and freeze and dry it, too / Daniel Gasteiger.
    p. cm.
  Includes index.
  ISBN 978-1-59186-487-5 (pbk.)
  1. Canning and preserving. 2. Food--Drying. 3. Frozen food. I. Title.
  TX603.G37 2010
  641.4'2–dc22

2010034939

First printing 2011
Printed in the United States of America
10 9 8 7 6 5 4 3 2 1

Managing Editor: Billie Brownell, Cover to Cover Editorial Services
Book Design: Mark Stephen Ross, Surfaceworks Design Studio
Cover Design: Marc Pewitt

Photography: *Daniel Gasteiger, pages: 5, 7, 8, 9, 11, 14, 17, 18, 20, 21, 22, 23, 24, 28, 30, 32, 33, 34, 36, 38, 39, 40, 43, 44, 45, 46, 47, 48, 50, 51, 52, 55, 56, 57, 58, 59, 60, 63, 64, 66, 67, 68, 70, 75, 76, 80, 81, 82, 83, 85, 86, 87, 88, 89, 92, 94, 96, 97, 99, 100, 102, 103, 104 107,108, 109, 110, 113, 114, 115, 116, 119, 120, 121, 124, 127, 134, 136, 137, 139, 142, 143, 147, 148, 150, 158,159, 160, 163,164, 165, 166,167, 170, 172, 173, 174, 177, 179, 180, 181,183, 184, 185, 186, 192, 194, 202, 203, 204, 205, 206, 208, 209, 214, 219, 220, 221, 224, 225, 227, 228, 230, 231, 233, 235, 236, 237.*

Thinkstock, pages: 2, 3, 4, 6, 10, 12, 13, 16, 19, 25, 26, 27, 29, 34, 37, 49, 54, 72, 73, 77, 78, 81, 82, 83, 84, 105, 117, 122, 128, 140, 141, 152, 157, 168, 198, 199, 200, 201, 216, 217, 234.

You can find this title, more Cool Springs Press books, and other gardening books for sale at *www.GardenBookstore.net.* Visit the Cool Springs Press website at *www.coolspringspress.com.*

Yes, You Can!

And Freeze and Dry It, Too

The Modern Step-by-Step Guide
to Preserving Food

Daniel Gasteiger

COOL SPRINGS PRESS

Growing Successful Gardeners™

BRENTWOOD, TENNESSEE

Acknowledgements

The following people and companies contributed in ways that were vital to the preparation of this book.

Thanks to Paul & Amy Underhill of Lewisburg, Pennsylvania, for supplying a range with a decent stovetop.

Thanks to The Metal Ware Corporation of Two Rivers, Wisconsin, for providing a NESCO American Harvest Dehydrator.

Thanks to Haupt Produce of Irish Valley, Pennsylvania, for giving me a tour of their cold storage facility and providing insights into modern produce production.

Thanks to The Melon Man Produce of Mount Joy, Pennsylvania, for providing some of the produce that appears in the book's photos.

Thanks to my wife and kids who reluctantly but patiently suffered surprise "taste attacks" (as in, "Taste this!") and endured months of a cluttered kitchen, dining room, porch, and basement as I shot photos for this book.

—Daniel

This book is for Mom, because she never had a book dedicated to her. I can still see her over the canning pot with a drop of sweat dripping off the tip of her nose.

This book is also for Dad, who managed to get his kids enthusiastic about gardening and farming without making it seem too much like work.

Finally, this book is for my gardening friends with whom I interact online through Twitter, Facebook, and many awesome blogs. Please join us all on Twitter. Find me at http://www.twitter.com/cityslipper, and I'll introduce you to the gang.

Table of Contents

Chapter **1**

Eat Better, Live Greener

Why Preserve Produce?

From a statistical perspective, Americans eat very poorly. We rely heavily on processed foods that contain too much salt and fat, artificial colors and flavors, and preservatives that have no nutritional value. It's sad that while these foods contribute to a burgeoning obesity problem, they are usually less expensive than fresh produce and unprocessed food products that are simply better for us.

The good news is that we have started to confront our bad dining habits. The Centers for Disease Control has identified obesity as a national health crisis, our government has launched an initiative for change, and a few popular television shows (such as *The Biggest Loser*) have raised awareness about the importance of improving our diets. More of us are rediscovering good food: we're buying fresh produce, frequenting farmers' markets, and even growing our own vegetables and fruit.

At the same time, living green is no longer an alternative lifestyle. Virtually every community sponsors at least some recycling, and many a company has found that going green can save money and boost the company's public image. At the grass roots level, the word is out that it's better to buy locally produced goods, and recently there has been a worldwide explosion of kitchen gardening.

Home food preservation can play an important role both in improving the quality of the food you eat and reducing your impact on the environment. When you preserve your own produce, you eat better and live greener.

Packaged processed foods seriously limit your options. Frozen meals, main courses, side dishes: there are just so many to choose from, and each one tastes exactly the way some industrial factory kitchen assembled it. Worse, whatever the packaging is—freezer pack, vacuum bag, can, or box—a commercial product undoubtedly contains preservatives, stabilizers, artificial colors, surfactants, emollients, emulsifiers, extra salt, or extra sugar. Do you want all that?

When you grow your own produce or buy it fresh from local sources, you have a pretty good idea of what's in that food. And when you can it, freeze it, dry it, or otherwise preserve it, you have a lot of control over the preservatives and other additives that go into it—if there are any at all.

Preserve Superior Flavor

Freshly harvested vegetables and the ones that you buy in a grocery store differ strikingly in flavor, texture, and nutritional content. This is partly true because commercial growers must plant varieties that store well and transport with minimal bruising.

A typical grocery store tomato is firm but relatively flavorless. You could grow similar tomatoes if you planted the varieties the commercial producers plant. However, you're more likely to grow tomato varieties that are juicy and flavorful and that bear almost no similarity to grocery store tomatoes. Homegrown peas are another amazing standout: you'll almost never find peas in a grocery store that taste as good as freshly harvested peas.

Even though home preservation methods involve cooking, freezing, and otherwise changing the characteristics of the food, freshly harvested vegetables and fruit retain much of that unique fresh-produce flavor when you preserve them yourself. What's more, many home-preserved foods have unique textures that you simply can't find in commercially preserved foods. A pear canned at home at the peak of ripeness, for example, is softer and naturally sweeter than a commercially canned pear.

I Can't Believe You Like That!

Because I was raised on home-canned peaches and pears, I always found the commercial equivalents to be hard and relatively flavorless. But when I first served home-canned peaches to my wife, she described them as being too soft.

You'll discover new textures when you preserve produce at home. In case you find some you don't like, start with small batches and simply steer away from the less pleasing ones as you increase your range of preserving skills. On the other hand, give yourself a chance to adjust, and after a season of eating home-preserved foods, you'll likely prefer them to the commercially preserved stuff.

Eat Better, Live Greener

Preserve Superior Nutrition

This may sound crazy but it's true: if you eat home-canned and home-frozen vegetables through the winter, you'll likely be eating more nutritious vegetables than if you buy "fresh" vegetables at the grocery store. That's because some vegetables can lose half their content of some vitamins just one or two days from harvest. So you can provide your family with better nutrition by preserving vegetables on the day you pick them from your garden or buy them at a local farmers' market.

Preserve the Environment

On average, the food you buy in a grocery store travels 1,500 miles to reach your table. It comes into the world from factory farms that operate huge machines and apply tons of chemicals to grow relatively high-quality produce.

Factory farms seem necessary when a society must feed cities housing millions of people. But people who can supply their kitchens from local growers and vendors significantly reduce their own impact on the environment. Buying from local growers at farmers' markets—even if those growers run factory farms—decreases the size of your carbon footprint. Of course, when you grow your own food, the decrease in your carbon footprint is dramatic.

We can buy "fresh" produce year-round all over the country because factory farms ship it everywhere.

But to rely only on local growers, you must buy produce in season and preserve it to consume during the winter. For people who live in temperate zones, it means giving up—or significantly reducing—"fresh" produce in the off season. This is easy to do; humankind has thousands of years of experience eating local fresh produce in season and storing extra to get through the winter. In fact, the very idea that you can eat lettuce during the deep cold of a northern winter is only a hundred or so years old.

Preserve Genetic Diversity

One great benefit of buying locally grown produce or, better still, growing your own, is that it supports genetic diversity of the world's food crops. Factory farms tend to grow varieties of fruits and vegetables that resist diseases, provide high yields, don't bruise easily, and can be planted and harvested by mechanical devices.

From one factory farm to the next, you'll find the same varieties of crops, and those appear reliably in your grocery stores. But here's the problem: if nearly every acre of tomatoes in a vast geographic area holds the Vine Ripe variety, that tomato type is extremely vulnerable. Suppose a new disease arises that thrives in Vine Ripe tomatoes and travels easily on the wind?

Imagine that instead of a "monoculture," the factory farms created a diverse culture of dozens of tomato varieties. The disease that damages Vine Ripe tomatoes might also damage five or six other varieties. However, growers might discover two or three dozen tomato varieties that are immune or resistant to that disease.

When you support local growers, they are able to plant varieties of fruits and vegetables that don't ship well; that practice simply wouldn't work on a factory farm. When you grow your own, of course, you can try all kinds of unusual crops that you'll never find in grocery stores.

By increasing the genetic diversity of the world's food supply, we lower its vulnerability to emergent diseases and plant-eating insects.

Local Favorites

While you can grow a diverse assortment of vegetables in just about any climate, certain vegetables seem to be fairly region specific. For example, the neck pumpkin is very common in central Pennsylvania. A neck pumpkin looks like a butternut squash on steroids. Some people call neck pumpkins "Pennsylvania Dutch crookneck squash," and through my blog and social networking I discovered that neck pumpkins are not common outside central Pennsylvania.

Despite neck pumpkin's popularity in Pennsylvania, few people, if any, use this squash for commercial production. You find it only at farm stands and farmers' markets late in the growing season.

When you buy from local food producers, you're likely to have access to regional favorites that never make it into grocery stores. More important, you're supporting growers who help maintain the genetic diversity of our food supplies.

Eat Better, Live Greener

Save Money When Food's on Sale

Even if you don't grow your own food, you can save a small fortune by preserving at home. One way to do this is to buy when produce is less expensive. Here are a few scenarios in which you can save:

• Produce that's in season locally may cost less than it does throughout the rest of the year—especially if it's a great growing season.

• A supermarket might put your favorite fruit or vegetable on sale to attract people into the store.

• A vendor with extra produce on hand (such excesses could be the result of purchasing bonuses, ordering errors, or bartering to smooth over mistakes) might prefer to sell it at cost or lower rather than toss it.

• Vendors at one-day markets (farmers' markets, growers' markets, flea markets) sometimes lower prices in the final hour or so of the day. They'd rather not load produce back on the truck.

• Some vendors pick out bruised, misshapen, or blemished produce and offer it as "pick-outs" or "windfalls" at significantly reduced prices.

• Some of a vendor's produce might be perfectly ripe, so the vendor offers a discount to encourage people to take it home before it starts to spoil.

• A farm or orchard might sponsor "you pick" hours, during which you can harvest produce at a substantial discount from the "already picked" price.

• A vendor might throw in some extra produce when you buy a lot all at once.

• A vendor who must sell whatever comes from the supplier—even bruised and damaged produce—might sell at considerably lower prices than you'd pay at a grocery store. Of course, you'll get some less-than-ideal produce in the transaction, but you'll probably get a bargain along with it.

Most of these scenarios are likely to arise at farmers' markets and farm stands. So to get your best produce deals, choose such vendors over supermarkets.

Dollars & Sense

Some Awesome Produce Buys

In season, blueberries in my town have run from $3 to $4 per quart over the past few years. Out of season, blueberries from Chile might cost $3 per cup!

Typically, we'll pay $3 or more for a pineapple at our local farmers' market. However, in early spring the price drops. For several months we can buy pineapples for $1.50, and I've even bought them for $1 apiece.

In season, a half bushel of apples might cost $8 to $12 from a local grower. However, the same grower sells half bushels of pick-outs for $5 or $6, depending on the variety of apple.

One of the most amazing produce buys I find weekly is at a local flea market: a vendor sells about 6 pounds of very ripe bananas for $1 (17¢ a pound)—their almost ripe bananas sell for 33¢ a pound.

Save by Making Your Own

Some prepared foods are very expensive. Spices, for example, can cost $3 to $5 a bottle for relatively small amounts. Some dried fruits sell for more than $5 per pound. With a dehydrator, or even just a dry space for hanging, you can fill spice bottles with your own dried herbs. And with a dehydrator or a carefully managed oven, you can make dried fruit snacks that taste better—and have fewer additives—than what you'd typically find in a grocery store.

Unless you're preserving homegrown produce, it's a little harder to argue you'll save money by canning applesauce, tomato sauce, spaghetti sauce, salsa, jam, jelly, or other highly processed foods. For some of these items, you may only shave pennies off the cost per quart if you make them from store-bought produce. And if you can find commercially manufactured jam and jelly for a few dollars per pint, you're not likely to make it cheaper at home.

However, don't let this financial consideration stop you. As you'll see, there are other good reasons to preserve your own foods.

Create Unique Flavors by Making Your Own

There are only so many food products available commercially, and can you really say that you've found the perfect salsa, the finest jelly, or the most curiously satisfying relish? When you learn to preserve your own foods, you can choose from a new palette of sauces, relishes, pickles, sauerkrauts, jams, jellies, and dried fruits, and tweak them to satisfy your own tastes.

My mom long ago discovered a recipe for chili sauce (page 234) that I make faithfully to top off meatloaf or fold into omelets. My mother-in-law discovered a recipe for red pepper relish (page 235) that tastes great on hors d'oeuvres and can also season a roast. I've developed a marinade for three-bean salad (page 236) that uses the "waste" juices from my mother-in-law's red pepper relish recipe. None of these items is available in stores.

As you try proven recipes, you can modify them within limits (for home canning, it's important not to stray far from USDA-tested products) and come up with family classics all your own.

When you learn to preserve your own, you can prepare large batches from favorite recipes using high-quality, locally grown ingredients and have them on hand year-round.

Surviving the Seasons

If your motive for preserving food is to save money, your food-preserving strategy may be as simple as always being ready to process food when the opportunity strikes. For example, citrus fruits don't grow where I live, but they're available in stores and at farmers' markets year-round. The best bargains for oranges, grapefruits, and tangerines come in late winter and early spring. If I buy in bulk then and preserve the citrus fruits, I won't be

When choosing the foods you'll preserve, focus on products that you use a lot.

tempted to pay two or three times as much
for "fresh" fruits during the off-season.

However, if you're going to live on
homegrown or local produce, you need a more
sophisticated strategy: you need to preserve the
produce you'll consume from the final local
harvest of fall through the first local harvests
of spring. Of course, what's in season in
spring isn't necessarily in season in autumn,
so preserves might need to last seven or eight
months, depending on your food preferences.

When planning for food preservation,
start by asking yourself this question: how
much of the food that I could preserve do
I usually eat? Cooking for my family of
five, I average about a pint of tomato sauce
per week. For some meals that use tomato
sauce, I might use a quart, and for other
meals I use about a cup, but there are many
weeks in which I use no tomato sauce.

Eat Better, Live Greener

I have a gardening friend who reports she uses a quart of tomato sauce pretty much every time she cooks with it, and she serves pasta with tomato sauce several times a week. So my friend cans more than fifty-two quart jars of tomato sauce each year. I can forty-eight pint jars of sauce (I don't use canned sauce during tomato season).

Applesauce is another story. One of my kids eats applesauce with nearly every meal, polishing off about a quart per week. Occasionally, the rest of us have applesauce and guests also dig into it. So I like to can fifty-two quart jars or more of applesauce (it makes no difference in flavor to eat applesauce fresh or canned). If we don't eat all the applesauce at meals, I substitute it for oil when I make bread.

The point is, I can't tell you how much of any produce to preserve. The most reliable way to come up with measurements is to track what you eat for a few months and make some assumptions based on that. Do you serve broccoli once a week or every night? Are potatoes your only or main dinner starch? Does your family consume five peanut butter and jelly sandwiches a day, or three per week? Do you make jellyrolls and jelly omelets? To how many people will you give jars of jams, jellies, relishes, or pickles?

How Much Should You Plant?

Are you planning to live year-round off homegrown produce? This is a bigger job than it may seem. If you were to calculate all the produce a family of five eats in one year, the amount would be staggering. Growing all of that yourself—and then preserving half of it—is a huge task. One of a family's primary functions used to be growing and putting up produce for itself. Of course, that same family grew grains, raised animals for meat, and provided for itself in dozens of other ways.

Realistically, you'll use homegrown fruits and vegetables to supplement your grocery shopping. A fine strategy is to focus first on vegetables and fruits you love, and grow as much of them as you can reasonably manage. The key concept is "reasonably manage."

Your Best Guess Is Wrong

My wife eats bananas straight from the peel. My kids and I eat bananas only after cooking them into banana bread. However, the first time I took a load of dried banana slices out of the food dehydrator, the kids and I devoured them in a day. Now when I slice up six pounds of bananas and dry them, they vanish in an afternoon.

Had I planned a year's consumption of dried bananas based on the number of bananas we eat in a month, I'd have been short by a few dozen gallons.

Your estimates are likely to be way off when you first start preserving food at home. Two factors are texture and habit.

Texture. New textures you discover when you preserve fruits and vegetables may lead you either to reject the preserved versions or to eat more of them. Of course, you might eat exactly as much of a preserved food as you would eat of the fresh food.

Habit. When my wife ran the kitchen and I preserved fruits and vegetables from my garden, the preserved stuff rarely showed up in our meals. My wife habitually shopped for certain things, and it never occurred to her to check the deep freeze or the larder. I also seem to be freezer challenged: six to ten fruit pies might sit in our freezer for nine months before I finally start serving them for desserts in the month before fruit season begins.

Make a reasonable estimate of how much to preserve, and notice when you run out—or if you have a whole bunch left when the next harvest begins. It will probably take a few years of preserving before you know just how much to put up.

Eat Better, Live Greener

It can take three to five potato plants to produce 5 pounds of potatoes. Some planting methods can trick plants into producing more.

You may be well equipped to freeze vegetables and can fruit, for example, but if you don't have a good cold-storage alternative, you should probably not emphasize root crops such as potatoes and carrots in your garden.

The estimates on the chart on the facing page work pretty well in my garden (I did math based on what I grow), but your soil, sunlight, moisture, and length of growing season will affect your crop yields, as will many other variables.

A Brief Comparison of Preservation Methods

Yes, You Can! covers many methods for preserving produce. There is no best method. Except for cold storage, every preservation technique changes the characteristics of the food it preserves. The following overview briefly describes each preservation method and the characteristics of foods preserved using that method; it also provides recommendations for ways to use the preserved foods.

These general observations will help you plan a produce garden to get you through a year, assuming you're feeding a family of five. Measurements describe rows or the number of seedlings to plant.

FOOD	MEALS	PLANTS
Beans (green or wax)	52	130 plants

Bean yield depends greatly on the variety of beans you grow and on how efficiently you harvest. Bush beans tend to produce two or three harvests per plant and then the plant dies. Climbing beans tend to produce through the end of the season.

FOOD	MEALS	PLANTS
Broccoli	52	40 plants

The first cutting from a broccoli plant might stretch for two meals. Left in the garden, the plant will continue to send up stems that produce smaller, but harvestable, heads. Forty plants should produce enough for one meal per week.

FOOD	MEALS	PLANTS
Cabbage	52	20 plants

Between cold-stored heads and canned or frozen sauerkraut, will you eat cabbage at least once a week? Raw cabbage heads of small varieties may provide enough for only two meals, while heads of larger varieties can easily cover five meals. With fermenting and cooking, the yield shrinks.

FOOD	MEALS	PLANTS
Carrots	52	43 feet

Assuming you thin to 2 inches between plants, you'll grow 260 carrots in 43 feet of row. Figuring five full-grown carrots per meal, you get a bump during the growing season as you consume young carrots you harvest while thinning your rows.

FOOD	MEALS	PLANTS
Peas	52	130 feet

Pea yield depends on the variety of peas you plant and the quality of support you provide for them. Many varieties will climb 4 to 6 feet on trellises, while others grow only 18 inches. It may take twenty-five or more plants to produce enough peas for one meal, but those peas will ripen over the course of two to six weeks.

FOOD	MEALS	PLANTS
Potatoes	52	78 plants

It's disappointing to dig a potato plant and find only two or three potatoes of significant size, but it happens. If your family eats five potatoes in a sitting and you serve potatoes weekly, you'll need to plant far more than one plant for each week of the year.

FOOD	MEALS	PLANTS
Winter squash	52	14 hills

Butternut, the most popular winter squash, is unpredictable. A vine can produce five or six fruits, leading you to think all plants do the same. However, one season I averaged 4¼ fruits per hill and each hill had two plants. Fourteen hills of butternut squash should provide one squash per week.

Eat Better, Live Greener

Averaging numbers from several sources, I've created a table that suggests how many row-feet to plant if you want to grow one meal's worth of vegetables for each week of the year. The table assumes spacing between plants according to typical planting instructions on the seed packages.

VEGETABLE	FEET
Asparagus	354
Beans, green or wax	200
Beans, lima	562
Beets	69
Broccoli	148
Cabbage	38
Carrots	50
Cauliflower	91
Corn	125
Cucumbers	62
Onions	37*
Peas	270
Peppers, bell	75
Potatoes	43
Radishes	126
Spinach	118
Summer squash	66
Sweet potatoes	50
Tomatoes	35**
Turnips	63
Winter squash	50

*Plant twice as many onions so you'll have plenty for seasoning dinners.

**Tomatoes lose volume when you prep them for storage. Also, you use an enormous amount of tomatoes to make sauces. So plant at least double this estimate if you're going to can or freeze tomato products.

COLD STORAGE

Some produce—roots, tubers, members of the onion family, and winter squashes— have natural staying power. Many keep well in a very cool, vaguely damp environment while others do better in a cool, dry setting. The important factor is "cool."

Through cold storage, you can convince these vegetables to stay "fresh" for many months. In fact, I buy potatoes from a local grower who stores tons of potatoes in cold, dark rooms and sells the previous autumn's crop all the way through June.

When cold storage works, you can have produce that appears and acts fresh months after the growing season ends. You can use cold-stored foods as you would use just-harvested produce.

Eat Better, Live Greener

DEHYDRATION

top bags is effective, and vacuum sealing them gives them a nearly infinite lifespan. Dehydrated foods are lightweight and easily portable, so they're very convenient when you need mobile food stores.

For nearly all dehydration, I encourage you to invest in a dedicated food dehydrator. A good one lets you control the temperature at which your food dries, and ensures you'll have satisfactory results. To dehydrate fruit, treat it with ascorbic acid or lemon juice if necessary (to keep it from changing color too badly), and then load it into the dehydrator. To dry vegetables, blanch or cook them and then put them in the dehydrator. Depending on the food, it can take twelve or more hours to drive out all the moisture.

Dehydrated fruits become new foods with textures and flavors that are quite different from those of the fresh versions. You might eat dehydrated fruits as snacks or incorporate them into baked goods, but unless you cook them, rehydrating isn't really an option.

Removing water from produce stops nearly all the chemical activity in the food. Produce shrivels as it dries and it loses weight. In fact, dehydrating can reduce a vegetable to one-fifth of its original size. You can protect dehydrated foods from spoilage simply by keeping them away from moisture; sealing them in zipper-

Vegetables lose their appeal when you dehydrate them. However, it's pretty common to cook vegetables, and most rehydrate very well. It's very unlikely that people will notice that the vegetables in casseroles, one-skillet meals, soups, or stews come from your store of dehydrated produce.

Canning Just Wasn't Enough

I grew up in a household with a deep freezer in the basement. My mother canned and my dad made wine. Preserving food for long-term storage was the rule at our house.

I've had a deep freezer as long as I've been married, and I started canning jam, jelly, and tomatoes when I settled in a house where I could plant a garden. Making jam and jelly is somewhat meditative for me: you must stir constantly or disaster may ensue. Still, canning wasn't enough.

Vegetables in my garden would ripen in big batches, and I learned to blanch and freeze peas, beans, and broccoli so they wouldn't end up growing mold in our refrigerator's vegetable drawer. Seduced by gorgeous fruit in season, I'd buy way too much and end up freezing fruit pies to eat through the year. Still, canning and freezing weren't enough.

One season, my peas got away from me and I let them dry on the vines, figuring I'd harvest them dry and cook them in a legume soup later. I discovered my toaster oven has a "dehydrate" setting, and I dried bananas, strawberries, and tomatoes that made amazing snacks for many weeks after harvest. Still, canning, freezing, and dehydrating weren't enough.

I discovered quick pickling and made dill pickles using vegetables and herbs from my garden. Now I save money by using home-pickled vegetables in my sweet-and-sour pork. Still, canning, freezing, dehydrating, and quick pickling weren't enough.

I think I've made my point: preserving produce at home can take on a life of its own. I've yet to tackle a preservation project that was overly challenging. Mostly, preserving food is about prepping fruits and vegetables and following simple procedures that are no harder than cooking a meal. I hope you catch my enthusiasm and learn all of the preservation methods I've written about in this book.

FREEZING

Once you cook something, it's a pretty good bet that it'll freeze well. This makes freezing the fallback preservation method for just about everything. However, more typically you freeze fruits or vegetables raw or partially cooked so you can use them out of season as if they're fresh. I say "as if" because freezing changes the texture of produce.

As produce freezes, ice forms inside its cells, causing many of them to burst. When you thaw the produce, it becomes limp or mushy. Frozen fruits work best in fruit salads or in foods such as milk shakes where you'll pulverize them anyway. Frozen vegetables require very brief cooking and offer a reasonable substitute for fresh-cooked vegetables in most dishes.

Freezing fruit involves putting it into containers, sometimes with sugar, and then storing it in the deep freezer. When you freeze

vegetables, you must first blanch them in boiling water and then freeze them.

The obvious drawback to freezing as a method of preservation is that it relies on electricity and a dedicated storage device to keep the food frozen. You can't easily take frozen food on the road, and if the electricity fails, you'll lose preserved food.

CANNING

You can preserve just about any produce through canning. What's more, the United States Department of Agriculture recommends you can foods that you've already preserved using other methods such as sugaring, fermenting, or quick pickling.

Canning cooks food inside of jars. The cooking kills microorganisms, destroys enzymes, and forces air out of the jars. The food, now in an oxygen-free bath, will keep for a year or longer at room temperature. That's convenient because canned food remains edible even if your electricity fails. Unfortunately, canning jars are bulky and heavy, so moving them can be a challenge.

Most fruits, including tomatoes, contain a lot of acid. When raised to the boiling temperature of water, that acid kills microbes and preserves the fruit. Vegetables contain very little acid and so must cook at a much higher temperature to ensure the microbes die. To can vegetables, you use a pressure canner, which raises the cooking temperature of your canning jars well above the boiling point of water.

While pressure canning low-acid foods is easy to do properly, it requires specialized equipment that you don't need for canning high-acid foods in a boiling water bath. In fact, a lot of canning-related activity has to do with adding acid to vegetables so you can process them safely in a boiling water bath canner.

For most of the canning projects in this book you'll use a boiling water bath canner—or you can use a large pot. But when you want to can vegetables more or less in their natural condition (ready to heat and serve), you'll need a pressure canner.

SUGARING

I adapted the word "sugaring" from the maple syrup industry. I mean it to refer to the act of adding sugar to foods to keep the food from spoiling. Jam, jelly, and syrup are examples of sugared foods. Our ancestors made these products to preserve fruit and fruit juice without canning or refrigeration—microbes don't grow well in sugar (they will grow if there's enough moisture). Today we can most sugared products to provide extra safety against harmful microbes.

Making jam, jelly, and syrup involves preparing fresh fruit or fruit juice, cooking it with lots of sugar, and putting it into jars to process in a boiling water bath canner. Of course, jams and jellies are great on peanut butter and jelly sandwiches, but they are also terrific components in baked goods and marinades, and they are delicious dessert toppings.

Eat Better, Live Greener

I like to mix homemade jam into yogurt or cottage cheese for an afternoon snack.

Preserved jams, jellies, and syrups have the same advantages and limitations as any canned products. On one hand, they don't require refrigeration. On the other hand, they're bulky and breakable and it's not practical to transport a large supply of canned goods if you need to move.

FERMENTATION

Fermentation produces lactic acid, which is a food preservative. You can ferment any vegetable or fruit. To ferment vegetables, submerge them in salt-water brine and let them sit for two to six weeks, depending on the temperature. The salt kills or suppresses molds, bacteria, and other microbes that might spoil the vegetables,

but the bacteria that produce favorable lactic acid fermentation don't mind it.

Historically, pickles were solely the product of this type of fermentation. (Sauerkraut and kimchi also develop in fermentation containers.) People would start the fermentation process in autumn and take out what they needed for meals until the vegetables were gone. Today, the USDA recommends that you can or freeze fermented vegetables when they've reached peak flavor—usually two to six weeks after you start the fermentation process.

Fermentation dramatically changes the texture and flavor of produce. Vegetables soften and develop a tangy flavor that some people don't care for. Eaten raw, fermented vegetables provide probiotics, whose benefits have recently come to the attention of health and natural foods enthusiasts.

When you cook fermented vegetables, you may wish to soak them and pour off the water to reduce their saltiness. They make great side dishes and can be delicious as ingredients in casseroles. Raw, they're great as salads and condiments—consider, for example, the iconic hotdog with sauerkraut.

Fermentation's obvious advantage is that it extends the life of produce at room temperature with no cooking required. However, you don't fully seal a fermentation container; carbon dioxide must be able to escape as the food ferments. This makes fermenting food very challenging to move around. Even after you can fermented vegetables, they offer the same storage and transportation challenges as any canned foods.

QUICK PICKLING

Vinegar is a product of fermentation. In fact, if you add salt to vinegar, you create something very much like the acidic brine that results from fermenting vegetables. This provides an awesome shortcut to pickling foods: immerse them directly in vinegar—or in brine that contains enough vinegar—and they won't spoil! That's the basic procedure involved in quick pickling.

With quick pickling, you cut up vegetables or fruit, cook brine that contains vinegar, and can the vegetables together with the brine. Through the selection of vegetables and the addition of sugar, salt, and seasonings, you can create a huge variety of pickles and relishes, all acidic enough for processing in a boiling water bath canner.

As with fermenting, quick pickling significantly changes the flavors and textures of the produce. In fact, quick pickling is more about recipes to produce specific products than it is about preserving vegetables to use later in cooking. You could conceivably create quick-pickled relishes and sauces whenever you wanted to use them, but it's more efficient and practical to make big batches while produce is in season, and then serve them when you wish.

LET'S GET STARTED!

With so many methods of preserving food, it can be challenging to choose a first project. I hope you'll read this entire book so you're familiar with all the ways to put up produce for long-term storage. However, if you want to jump in with a project that provides near-instant gratification, I recommend that you make jam or jelly.

To prepare, read Chapter 5 through the section "Basic Steps for Boiling Water Bath Canning." Then skip ahead to Chapter 6, which introduces sugaring and then talks you through your first jam-making session.

I'll take you through it all, step by step!

Chapter 2

Cold Storage

Year-Round Fresh Food

Can you harvest fresh vegetables in autumn and keep them fresh well into the next spring, or even summer? Yes, you can, but you have to harvest the right vegetables. Amazingly, you don't need high-tech climate control or chemical preservatives to make certain foods last in good condition for many months.

Root crops such as potatoes, carrots, yams, turnips, beets, parsnips, and rutabagas all have considerable staying power under the right conditions. Alliums—onions, leeks, and garlic—prefer slightly different conditions, but they also will keep for a surprisingly long time. Squashes are a third category of vegetables that you can consume as "fresh" many months after you harvest them, and even cabbage will keep well into winter if you store it properly.

Under the right conditions some fruits will remain good to eat for several months—nearly indistinguishable from freshly harvested fruit. Many apples you find in grocery stores in December and January, for example, went into cold storage the previous October or November. I don't advocate storing your own fruit this way (for best results, suppliers count the days from when the trees blossom, harvest the fruit green, and store it at 30 to 32 degrees Fahrenheit), but the point is this: some fresh produce can remain "fresh" for a very long time.

Cold Storage

Your Great-Grandma's Produce Drawer

If you miss a potato when you harvest and it stays in the ground through the winter, chances are good that it will sprout in the spring. Our ancestors must have noticed this, because they realized that buried potatoes remained relatively fresh for many months. What better inspiration could there have been to invent the root cellar?

A root cellar has several important characteristics:

- It is dark.
- It is heavily insulated, usually by surrounding soil.
- It has a means for letting in cold air, when necessary.
- It can retain high humidity in the air.

For me, the words root cellar conjure images of my childhood neighbor's dark, cool, dirt-floored basement. There under a single dim light bulb was a hip-deep wooden bin filled with sandy soil. Buried in that bin were potatoes and carrots, and probably other root vegetables as well.

For some families, a root cellar was simply a hole in the ground with a cover. I've spoken with people who remember their parents going out to the "cave," lifting the cover, and dragging out produce to cook for dinner.

Other root cellars, like my friend's, were no more than basement rooms with dirt floors, bins of soil, and a window that their owners would open periodically to cool the space. Still others were small shelters, separate from the house and well submerged in the soil.

Cold Stores More Than Root Vegetables

Potatoes, carrots, beets, parsnips, and rutabagas love cold storage with high humidity—the kind of atmosphere it's easy to maintain in an old-fashioned root cellar. If you have a cold, damp basement, you might be able to store these vegetables for many months and continue to eat them "fresh." Coincidentally, cabbage also likes a cold, moist environment and will keep for five months or more in a root cellar.

On the other hand, onions and garlic like an environment that's cold and dry. Kept near freezing with low humidity, these vegetables can last for four months. Pumpkins and winter squash will also last a long time in cold storage, but they prefer a cool, dry environment (around 55 degrees Fahrenheit) rather than one that's cold and dry.

So if you want to experiment with cold storage, first evaluate your living and storage spaces: is there a place in your house that stays around 55 degrees Fahrenheit year-round; an area that you can wall in and insulate, and hold at a low temperature by periodically opening a window on cold winter days?

Why No Refrigeration?

If all these vegetables store so well at cool or cold temperatures, why not use modern refrigeration to keep them through the winter months? Sustainability. Modern refrigeration consumes electricity and can fail for reasons beyond your control.

By using the earth as an insulator and winter cold as their cooling system, many commercial growers maintain tons of stored root crops that they send to market throughout the winter. If your family consumes 10 pounds of potatoes per week, you need to store only 290 pounds (assuming 4½ weeks for each month) for 7 months to make it through the nongrowing season!

Cold Storage

From the Tip Jar

The temperatures in southern climes may not be ideal for maintaining a cold storage facility without refrigeration. But even a cool storage space can extend the life of your produce. For example, butternut squash lasts for about five months on my dining room floor, and the temperature there never drops below 65 degrees Fahrenheit. Still, in some climates, it's more practical to rely on other preservation methods for your root vegetables, winter squash, onions, and cabbage.

Your Own Cold Storage

When creating a cold-storage facility, consider the presence of insects and rodents. Most of us don't want such critters in our living spaces, and it's even more unpleasant to discover them in our food. If you're not confident that your house will keep rodents out, your storage bins can serve that purpose. Unfortunately, you can't rely on storage bins to lock out insects because cold-stored foods must have air movement to stay fresh.

You don't need to be a carpenter to create a decent cold store. You can install plastic bins and shelving units in a cool basement room. Ideally, the room will have a window that you can open periodically on cold autumn nights and throughout the winter to reduce the temperature of that room. However you lay out a cold-storage room, hang a thermometer and a barometer to monitor temperature and humidity to help you establish good habits about managing the environment.

Cold, Moist Storage

32 to 40 degrees Fahrenheit
90 to 95 percent humidity

Potatoes, carrots, beets, parsnips, rutabagas, and cabbages need a humid, cold environment. A damp basement room may provide the necessary humidity, and you can simply stack root vegetables on the floor, on shelves, or in open bins. If your basement is dry, you can add moisture to the cold-storage bins.

Set large plastic storage bins on the floor and cover the bottoms with an inch of damp sand (or sawdust or peat moss). If you use sand, the product sold as "playground sand" will leave the skins of the vegetables a bit cleaner. Then add a layer of the vegetable you're storing, fill with damp sand until you cover those vegetables, add another layer of vegetables, fill with damp sand, and so on until you've filled the containers. For best results, don't let the vegetables touch each other (when they touch, a vegetable that spoils can more easily cause its neighbor to spoil too).

Moistening the packing material—whether sand, sawdust, or peat moss—before putting it in the storage bin prevents you from accidentally getting the bin so wet that water pools in the bottom.

Packing Materials for Cold Storage

While I encourage you to use sand to pack root vegetables for cold storage, other materials will work as well. If you have a convenient supply of sawdust, use that, or get some peat moss instead. In all cases, moisten the packing material before you load it into your storage bins with vegetables.

When you've used the vegetables from the bins, compost the sawdust or peat moss that you used in packing—or apply it as mulch. These materials tend to deteriorate over time, particularly when they're damp. It doesn't hurt to haul sand outdoors and let it dry out thoroughly between seasons, but this isn't a common practice; people routinely bury produce in the same material for years without refreshing it.

Cold Storage

If you have concerns about rodents, cover these containers, but drill dozens of holes in the lids (use a drill bit that's smaller than the diameter of a pencil). Or cut the center out of the lid and use the modified lid to hold a piece of nylon window screen or other tight-woven mesh on the container. If you block the airflow to your produce, you'll shorten its shelf life.

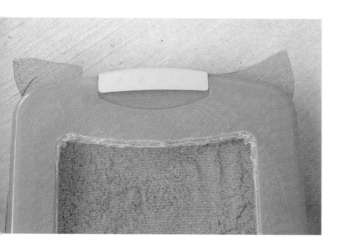

While carrots, beets, parsnips, rutabagas, and cabbage will keep longest in a room at 32 to 34 degrees Fahrenheit, this is a problem for potatoes. Potatoes won't spoil, but the starch in them will change to sugar. During frying, that sugar may brown too quickly, resulting in crispy or dark fried potato products. The ideal temperature for storing potatoes is 38 to 40 degrees Fahrenheit.

Cold, Dry Storage
32 to 34 degrees Fahrenheit
65 to 70 percent humidity

Creating a cold, dry storage facility in a damp basement is a true engineering challenge. Dehumidifiers tend to heat the air in a room, so if you want to dry out a damp basement room, install an air conditioner.

On the other hand, if you want to eliminate dependence on electricity, seal the walls and the floor of the basement room with waterproofing paint. Then rely on climate to dry the room.

Fortunately, cold winter air is usually quite dry. So when you open the window of your damp basement room to cool it down, you'll also reduce the room's humidity. That may be enough to keep onions happy. Then, as atmospheric humidity increases in spring, move whatever onions you haven't consumed into your refrigerator.

You've hit the mother lode of cold-storage potential if you have a windowed basement room that stays relatively dry. You can use plastic bins filled with moist sand to hold root vegetables and cabbages, and then hang onions, garlic, and leeks from the walls or ceiling—or put them in baskets on shelves. With adequate air circulation, moisture in the storage bins won't significantly humidify the air in the room.

Cool, Dry Storage

50 to 55 degrees Fahrenheit
60 to 80 percent humidity

Finding a place to store pumpkins and winter squash can be as easy as putting them out of the way. You can store them in any room in a dry basement and they should keep well through the winter.

If your basement is damp, find the coolest dry room in the house and the squash will be okay there. For several years, I've carelessly left a pile of butternut squash on the floor of our dining room in October, and we've eaten it as late as mid-March.

Ideally, store pumpkins and squash in a single layer so they don't touch each other. When selecting squash for a meal, use any that show signs of shriveling or discoloration first.

Manage Produce from Harvest to Spring

If you had to guess how to prepare produce for cold storage, you'd probably get decent results. However, to ensure the best possible food store throughout the winter, use these tips when preparing your harvest for cold storage.

• Harvest vegetables that are ready to eat and reject any that show insect damage or disease.

• Don't scratch or bruise the produce before putting it in storage.

Traditional Cold Stores

Root cellars are, perhaps, the easiest sustainable cold-storage facilities for the typical homeowner to create. Closely related to the root cellar is the springhouse, which is a structure built over a spring, a stream, or an open well where cold water and evaporating moisture provide cooling.

A farmer would sometimes build a summer kitchen. Detached from the farmhouse, the summer kitchen was a place to cook without introducing more heat to the living space. The ideal summer kitchen sat on a stream or spring, which provided cold storage right where one would prepare a meal.

Perhaps the most elaborate cold-storage strategy predating electricity was the icehouse. In winter, the owner of an icehouse would cut blocks of ice from a nearby frozen river, lake, or pond and stack them tightly inside. Ice stored this way might last until July or August, not only providing cold storage for produce, but also providing ice to cool drinks and make ice cream.

• Use varieties of vegetables that mature late in the year. One of the great challenges of preserving produce through cold storage is keeping it in good condition until your storage facility is cold enough. With late-maturing crops, you'll be harvesting as nights get cold.

• Before packing, thoroughly wash crops that require cold, moist storage. Soil and other residue might contain microbes that could spoil the food.

Cold Storage

Cold-Store Your Canned Goods

If you establish a cold-storage space to hold root vegetables, onions, and cabbage in your house, you're creating an ideal place to keep canned goods. In fact, root cellars often had walls of shelves loaded with canned goods in the fall; by late spring, these shelves would be lined with empty jars awaiting the next harvest.

BEETS: COLD, MOIST

Harvest beets when they're 1¼ to 3 inches across. Wash the beets and remove their tops before loading them into containers for storage. Beets will remain fresh for up to 5 months.

CABBAGE: COLD, MOIST

Harvest heads of any size once they've tightened up. Cut the stem flush and remove loose leaves. Wrap each cabbage in newspaper before storing in a container; the newspaper will prevent packing sand from getting into the cabbage. Cabbages can stay fresh for up to 5 months.

CARROTS: COLD, MOIST

Harvest mature, firm carrots before they send up flower stalks. Cut the tops off close and wash the carrots before packing them for storage. Carrots may retain their quality for 8 months.

GARLIC: COLD, DRY

Harvest garlic when the bottom three leaves wither. Use a garden fork to dig under the plants. Without washing them, set the plants to cure in a warm space with good airflow for 4 to 6 weeks. When the skins dry and harden, remove the outer layers, taking the dirt with them. Then braid the stalks for easy hanging or remove the stalks and load the hardened cloves into mesh bags or baskets. Garlic will remain fresh for up to 7 months.

ONIONS: COLD, DRY

Harvest onions after the stalks fall over and begin to dry; don't wash them. Let them cure at room temperature for 2 to 4 weeks. For a decorative look, braid the dried stalks together to hang. Ideally, if you are more interested in results than appearance, remove the stalks and place the onions in baskets or mesh bags before putting them in cold storage. Onions will remain fresh for up to 7 months.

PARSNIPS: COLD, MOIST

Harvest parsnips after a heavy frost by digging deep near the plants and working your way toward the roots. Remove the tops and wash the parsnips before packing for storage. Parsnips will stay fresh for 4 to 6 months.

POTATOES: COLD, MOIST

Harvest potatoes within a month of the plants dying back and before the soil temperature drops below 40 degrees Fahrenheit. Wash the potatoes before packing them for storage. Potatoes will remain fresh for up to 9 months.

RUTABAGAS: COLD, MOIST

Harvest rutabagas after a few frosts, mounding soil around exposed roots to prevent cold damage. Discard the tops and wash the rutabagas to remove soil before packing them in storage containers. Rutabagas will last for up to 4 months.

Cold Storage

WINTER SQUASH AND PUMPKINS: COOL, DRY

Harvest fully ripe squash and pumpkins, though if you pick them green, they will continue to ripen. Cure them in the sun for 10 to 14 days when the air temperature is 70 to 80 degrees Fahrenheit; don't leave them out overnight when they can get damaged by frost. If sun-curing isn't practical, store them indoors at room temperature for a few weeks.

Store squash or pumpkins in a single layer without contact between pieces. Winter squash and pumpkins will last for up to 6 months.

YAMS (SWEET POTATOES): COOL, DRY

Harvest yams before frost kills the vines. Cure yams for 10 days in a warm, moist environment of 80 to 85 degrees Fahrenheit. Store only the larger ones in baskets or breathable bags (paper or mesh). Yams remain fresh for up to 6 months.

Root Crops Provide Their Own Moisture

If you're lucky enough to have a damp root cellar, you can simply fill bins with your crops—you don't need special packing to keep the conditions humid. However, when you store a large heap of root vegetables, even in a fairly dry room the vegetables release enough moisture to humidify the space. Chemical activity in the root crops will produce heat, which will be greatest in the middle of the heap.

So if you have such a pile of produce, rearrange it from time to time to prevent the buried pieces from softening and starting to grow. To avoid this problem, commercial storage facilities run ventilation ducts through their potato bins to distribute cold air to the bottom of the heap and prevent the buried pieces from softening and starting to grow.

Chapter 3

When you're looking at fresh produce, it may be hard to imagine that drying it is a good way to preserve it. That's because fruits and vegetables contain a lot of moisture. In most cases, the moisture is what makes the produce firm, crisp, or crunchy. When you let vegetables dry out, they get soft and droopy and less appetizing.

However, dehydrated food is incredibly versatile. We use so many dehydrated products that we may not even recognize them as such. For example, you might find some of these dehydrated foods in your pantry:

Seasonings

Soup mixes

Coffee creamers and hot chocolate mixes

Pasta

Cornmeal

Tea leaves

Stuffing mixes

Fruit roll-ups

Jerky

Dried fruit (well, yeah!)

Simple, Natural Preservation

It may seem contrary to nature to preserve fresh produce by drying it, but dehydration is actually nature's way of saving food to feed animals in winter. Meadow grasses dry in place, providing hay for foraging mammals. Berries and fruits dry on the branches of bushes and trees to feed birds and rodents throughout the cold months.

Air-Dried Herbs

You don't need fancy equipment to dry your own herbs; people have been hanging herbs to dry for centuries. Air-drying has a couple of advantages:

- You can hang dozens of plants at once; you're not limited to drying what fits in a dehydrator.

- Air drying doesn't consume electricity.

The simplest approach to air-drying herbs is to stretch string in an out-of-the-way corner of just about any room that is out of direct sunlight (and preferably not in a damp basement). To dry annuals such as dill, cilantro, parsley, and basil, pull the plants by their roots, shake off the soil, and hang the plants tops-down on the string.

To dry perennial herbs where harvesting whole plants would be inappropriate, harvest the stems and tie them in bunches with lightweight twine. Then hang these bunches of herbs alongside the drying annuals.

It may take several weeks for some herbs to dry completely. When the leaves crumble easily and the stems are brittle, store them in zipper-top bags or other airtight containers. Or pulverize dried herbs in a blender and refill your spice jars with the resulting powders. (See page 55 for more about drying and storing herbs.)

Imagine the relief our ancestors must have felt in late winter to find desiccated cherries, apples, or grapes still clinging to their respective plants. The prehistoric genius who decided to gather and dry fruits, vegetables, and grains under controlled conditions and then store them away from foraging animals probably commanded the type of respect we reserve today for Thomas Edison and Albert Einstein.

They may not look appetizing, but grapes dried on the vine might have made a midwinter feast for our distant ancestors.

While you can still rely on prehistoric methods to dehydrate produce for long-term storage, modern methods are more reliable. Dedicated dehydrators maintain a constant temperature while moving air over the food to remove moisture. Even with no previous experience, everyone can succeed with a home dehydrator. You can also dry food in a conventional oven or a toaster oven.

The Dehydration Advantage

Dehydrated produce keeps very well in simple packaging: airtight zipper-top bags, jars with screw-on lids, plastic food-storage containers—pretty much any container that keeps air and moisture away from the food.

Dehydrated food is lightweight and, once packaged, it needs no special environment to remain edible. Ideally, you'll store dried foods in cool, dry places, but they don't require refrigeration or cold storage. So with a stock of dehydrated fruits and vegetables, you're prepared in the event of lengthy power outages during which frozen foods would melt and spoil.

Without the bulky glass jars you use in canning, dried foods are easier to manage and less prone to damage from being bumped or dropped. And while canning requires added water, resulting in increased weight, drying removes water, making your stores very light and easy to transport. Removing water from produce can reduce it to one-fifth of its original size, so if storage space is at a premium, get to work with a dehydrator.

Foods That Dehydrate Well

It's hard to name foods that don't dehydrate well. Fruits, vegetables, grains, herbs, and meats are all candidates for drying. Goodness, one of the most popular backpacking foods when I was a kid was freeze-dried ice cream—a product you can duplicate easily using a machine intended for in-home dehydrating.

Perhaps the more important issue to consider is how you will use the foods you dry. When you first get a dehydrator, it tempts you to load it up and set it drying. And when you find produce at deep discounts at farmers' markets or roadside stands, it's hard not to buy a few pounds for the dehydrator.

But what's the point of drying grapes, for example, if no one in your family craves raisins? At my house, I can't add raisins to baked goods unless I want leftover baked goods. I was pleasantly surprised when I found my family would devour dried bananas even though they never touch fresh bananas.

So before you dry every berry, bean, pineapple, or potato in sight, think about how you'll use the dried produce later on. Fruit leathers (roll-ups) may be an easy call, but dried asparagus or sweet potatoes could offer culinary challenges.

Fruits: Every fruit I've ever dried made good eating just the way it was. Among my favorites are dried bananas and seasoned dried tomatoes. I'm happy to snack on these in place of carbohydrate-heavy packaged snacks (and I *love* carbohydrate-heavy packaged snacks). But rehydrating dried fruits is only marginally successful. In most cases, if you simply float the dried bits in water, you'll end up with some pretty scary stuff.

So I suggest you dry fruits for snacking, and to use in cooking. Dried apricots, pineapple, apples, strawberries, plums, pears, melons, mangoes, grapes, cherries, blueberries, bananas, and kiwis all make fine snack foods on their own. But chunks of these also work very well in trail mixes and baked goods. Happily, they rehydrate appropriately when you use them in cooking.

Vegetables: We're probably most familiar with the dehydrated vegetables that come in soup-in-a-cup type packages. These might include tiny cubes of vegetables and powdery dried herbs. An advantage of drying your own vegetables is that you determine the sizes of the pieces. So if you want to save ingredients for a robust vegetable-laden soup, you might dehydrate large chunks of carrots, potatoes, turnips, beans, celery, and onions. Later these will rehydrate in soup broth and quite remarkably resemble the original vegetables.

There aren't as many dehydrated vegetables I'd eat as snacks as I do dried fruit. Actually, some are quite tasty but they tend to be very dry and unappetizing. Still, try dried (blanched) sweet corn for a crunchy snack, and you might be pleasantly surprised. Or slice potatoes, sweet potatoes, or squash thinly, then blanch and dehydrate. You might enjoy the resulting chips with dips and salsas.

Basic Steps to Drying Produce

Whether you're drying fruit, vegetables, herbs, or mushrooms, the steps are nearly identical. In all cases, you clean the produce and toss the bad stuff. You peel and core some fruits and vegetables and, usually, you cut the produce into smaller pieces—thin slices dry quicker than big chunks do. Finally, you let the produce dry.

Steps To Drying Produce

Step 1

Clean the drying trays and your work surfaces. Ideally, use a mild chlorine bleach solution (a teaspoon of bleach mixed with a quart of water) to sterilize cutting boards, countertops, and drying trays. Rinse thoroughly before you set food on them.

For most vegetables, blanch before dehydrating.

Color Changes in Dried Produce

When you dry fruits and vegetables, colors can change dramatically. Potatoes, for example, can turn black as they dry. Blanching vegetables before drying them nearly eliminates discoloration, so blanch according to the instructions on page 44.

To limit discoloration in dried fruit, soak prepared fruit pieces in a mild acid solution before putting them in the dehydrator. Apples, peaches, apricots, and pears are particularly susceptible to discoloration.

To make an acid solution, add ½ to ¾ cup bottled lemon juice to 1 gallon water. Alternatively, buy ascorbic acid powder (available in season with canning supplies at your grocery store or at a pharmacy), and mix 1 teaspoon ascorbic acid with 1 gallon water. As you skin, pit, and slice your fruit, drop the pieces in the solution and let them soak more than an hour before placing them onto trays for drying.

Prepare the produce. You'll find instructions for preparing many types of produce on page 53 and in other chapters of this book. For high-acid and high-sugar produce (specifically fruit), drying suspends biological activity and keeps the food from spoiling. However, for most low-acid produce (vegetables), drying alone doesn't stop enzymes in the food from continuing to work. Unchecked, the enzymes will make even dried produce continue to age; vegetables may change color and develop unappealing flavors. So for most vegetables, blanch before drying.

For berries and small vegetables such as peas, you can simply clean them and load them in the dehydrator. For large berries, fruits, and vegetables, clean them and slice them into segments about ½ inch thick. In some cases, you may want to shred the produce before drying, depending on how you expect to use it. Shredded potatoes, for example, rehydrate well for pan-frying.

Load the drying trays. You might have seen photographs of drying trays holding artistically arranged patterns of fruits or vegetables ready to load into a dehydrator. Insanity! Load your drying trays with produce any way you want; no one will be looking at them while they dry. I tend to put only one type of fruit or vegetable on each tray. Pack the produce, but don't overlap it unless it's something light such as herbs or shredded vegetables.

Blanching Basics

Blanching means cooking partially. One rule of thumb is to cook a vegetable for one-third of the time you would if you were going to serve it at a meal. Another rule of thumb is to cook a vegetable for half of the normal total cooking time. Such rules introduce potential problems: do you normally cook vegetables until they're very soft or until they have a crispy crunch? Because preferences vary, forget "normal" and blanch with two goals:

- Get the vegetables hot all the way through.
- Keep most blanched vegetables firm or even crisp—except in the case of winter squash, pumpkins, and potatoes. Blanch these vegetables until they are completely cooked.

Blanching in a Microwave Oven

To blanch vegetables in a microwave oven, fully prepare them for drying and put the pieces into a microwave-safe bowl. Cover the bowl and cook the vegetables on high according to the following list:

> Leafy vegetables: 2 to 3 minutes per pound
>
> Asparagus, celery, and eggplant: 3½ to 4 minutes per pound
>
> Green and wax beans, broccoli, cauliflower, and winter and summer squash: 4 to 5 minutes per pound
>
> Carrots, artichokes, radishes, potatoes, sweet potatoes, turnips, and parsnips (all sliced): 5 to 7 minutes per pound
>
> Corn (before removing from the cob): 4 minutes per pound
>
> Shredded vegetables (carrots, cabbage, onions, peppers, and zucchini) and peas: 2 to 3 minutes per pound

Blanching for Dehydration
The vegetables you blanch should go directly into your dehydrator; there's no need to cool them down rapidly first as you would for freezing.

About halfway through the blanching process, stir the vegetables to ensure even cooking.

Blanching on the Stovetop

To blanch vegetables for dehydration, don't submerge them in boiling water as you might for freezing. Rather, use a large pot with a lid that fits well, and position a wire basket or colander several inches above the bottom of the pot.

Put an inch or two of water in the pot and heat it to a rolling boil. Then put the prepared vegetables in the colander and put the colander in the pot. Start timing as soon as you cover the pot and cook for the following times:

Leafy vegetables: 3 minutes (4½ minutes for collard greens)

Asparagus, celery, and eggplant: 3 to 6 minutes

Green and wax beans, broccoli, cauliflower, and winter and summer squash: 3 to 6 minutes

Carrots, artichokes, radishes, potatoes, sweet potatoes, turnips, and parsnips (all sliced): 3 to 7½ minutes

Corn (before removing from the cob): 6 minutes

Shredded vegetables (carrots, cabbage, onions, peppers, and zucchini) and peas — 2½ minutes

Put each filled tray directly into the dehydrator set to its appropriate heat setting. For fruit, the temperature should be between 130 and 140 degrees Fahrenheit. For vegetables, use a temperature of 130 to 145 degrees Fahrenheit. For herbs, dry between 90 and 100 degrees Fahrenheit.

If you add fresh produce to the dehydrator along with partially dehydrated produce, separate them on different trays; the drying time will increase for all the produce in the dehydrator.

Step 5

Check the drying progress to determine whether your vegetables are ready for storage. If you anticipate 6 to 10 hours of drying time, check first after 6 hours and then check every hour or so until your produce is dry.

Step 6

Package your dried produce into airtight containers and label with the contents and the dates on which you packed them. For the longest storage, use a vacuum-packing system to remove air from your containers. Mix several types of fruits or vegetables in the same container only if you don't care that their flavors will intermix; dried bananas may pick up the flavors of strawberries and cherries, for example, if you package all three together.

Step 7

Store dried produce in a cool, dark place. Light, heat, and moisture will degrade the quality of dehydrated food. So, especially if you've packaged it in transparent containers, store dehydrated produce in a cabinet, a dark closet, or even in an opaque storage bin with a tight lid.

While you can dehydrate in any oven using a very low heat setting, you'll be glad if you invest in a dedicated machine.

You'll find several designs of dehydrators. They'll all dry fruits and vegetables adequately, but there are a few features that really streamline your efforts. You may spend a bit more for the perfect setup, but the reliability and time savings offset the cost very quickly.

A typical dedicated dehydrator consists of a set of trays that hold food while leaving gaps for air to move. An electric fan blows warm or hot air through the trays and the air emerges, carrying a bit of moisture with it. Some dehydrators simply heat and blow air around the food. Others include a thermostat that lets you set desired operating temperatures.

Many vegetables rehydrate sufficiently for you to serve them as if they were cooked fresh. (It's amazing to rehydrate dried yam disks, cook them up, and candy them. The result is indistinguishable from fresh candied yams.) All rehydrated vegetables perform very well in soups, sauces, stews, and other dishes in which vegetables typically serve as components rather than as the main ingredient.

For dehydrators to work efficiently, the trays must fit into a drying chamber. Some dehydrators are cabinets into which you slide the trays, ultimately closing the cabinet door to complete the drying chamber. Other dehydrators create a drying chamber as you stack trays of food on top of each other; the sides of the trays become the walls of the chamber.

Equipment for Dehydrating

To prepare fruits and vegetables for dehydrating, you need a vegetable peeler, paring knives, cutting knives, and a cutting surface. You must blanch vegetables before dehydrating them, so you also need a microwave oven and a large microwave-safe bowl with a cover or a large lidded pot to use on your stove.

Dehydration

Important Features to Consider

Batch-size versatility. It's nice to be able to dry small batches of food without dragging out a massive dehydrator. It's also nice to be able to dry twelve or more pounds of produce to speed production during a good harvest. Dehydrators that have cabinets in which you place food-holding trays obviously have a maximum load limit. But don't let the apparent expandability of stackable-tray dehydrators fool you: if you stack too many trays for a single load, your produce won't dry properly.

Wattage. A food dryer with high wattage can produce more heat and move more air than one with low wattage. A small dehydrator might have a 200-watt rating, while a large, expandable dehydrator might have a 700-watt rating. For stackable-tray dehydrators, investing in high wattage lets you dry more each time you run the device. For cabinet-style dehydrators that aren't expandable, trust the manufacturers to build in enough wattage to dry a full load.

Fine-screened food trays. For typical items such as halved cherries, broccoli spears, sliced onions, and pineapple chunks, a drying tray looks like a window screen with a fairly large weave. However, herbs, grains, and other small items may slip through the holes in a standard tray—particularly as the foods dry out and lose volume. NESCO, a popular manufacturer of food dryers, makes "microscreens" that fit on a standard drying tray and reduce the sizes of holes through which food might pass. Obtain a few similar screens made specifically for your food dryer.

Fruit leather pans. You can place plastic wrap on food-drying trays to produce fruit leathers, but using fruit leather pans or trays produces more consistent results. Most manufacturers make leather pans or trays to fit their dehydrators. Get some. You may not be a fan of fruit leathers yet, but experience using a dedicated dehydrator could quickly win you over.

Airtight storage containers. Dried fruits and vegetables keep amazingly well as long as you keep them dry. Humidity in the air softens them up and leads quickly to spoilage. So invest in rigid sealable containers or zipper-top bags to store dried produce. To maximize shelf life, use a vacuum-sealing system and store dried fruits and vegetables in air-free containers.

Jerky shooter. Jerky isn't for everyone, but if you like eating jerky, you might also enjoy making your own. A jerky shooter lets you make "Jerky sticks" similar to Slim Jims™; you mix ground meats and seasonings, and a jerky shooter shapes the mixture into jerky sticks or ribbons for the dehydrator.

Deli slicer. Though not essential, a deli slicer is a terrific device to have if you're going to make jerky. However, a deli slicer isn't appropriate for cutting up fruits and vegetables, so I'm not recommending it for any of the projects I describe in this book.

Amazing Crunchy Corn Snacks

With a few minutes work, you can create surprisingly fresh-tasting and delicious crunchy snacks that may become a family favorite.

Step 1

Select ears of your favorite variety of ripe, fresh sweet corn. Settle for nothing less quality-wise than ears you'd buy when serving corn on the cob.

Step 2

Husk the corn and steam blanch it for six minutes. (Find instructions for blanching vegetables on page 44.)

Step 3

Use a large knife to cut the corn from the ears. Doing this well takes practice. If you cut too deeply, you'll remove cob with the corn, and chewing that is most unpleasant. Shallow cuts clip corn kernels, leaving a lot of corn on the ear. But I would rather cut too little off the ears than too much.

Step 4

Spread the corn kernels on a microscreen or a lightly oiled fruit leather tray. Dry them at 130 to 140 degrees Fahrenheit for 6 to 12 hours.

Store these snacks in an airtight container, and serve them without guilt when your kids want snacks between meals.

In The Kitchen With DANIEL

Oven-Dried Produce

You can dehydrate produce in a conventional oven, but you'll need to experiment to find the right temperature setting and the most reliable arrangement of drying pans. It's easy to get the temperature too high, which will cook your produce before it dries.

Foods with high sugar content are likely to discolor as the sugar caramelizes. What's worse is that the texture of the produce changes when the sugar cooks. But when the oven isn't hot enough, microorganisms can grow on the produce. Because oven temperature settings are quirky at best, use a separate oven thermometer so you'll know which dial setting on your oven indicates the correct temperature for drying food.

Note, it costs more to heat a full-sized oven than it does to heat the drying chamber of a dedicated dehydrator. Because a dehydrator moves heated air about in the drying chamber, it is very efficient and cost-effective. You could use twice as much electricity to dry produce in an oven than in a dedicated dehydrator.

Testing for Dryness

Many fruits will dry until they're brittle, but that's not good. Instead, dry fruits only until they're stiff but flexible; after they've cooled, they shouldn't be sticky to the touch. Properly dried fruit is chewy. Think of the raisins, dates, and dried apricots that you've bought in a grocery store.

To test dryness in fruit, remove a piece from the dehydrator, let it cool, and then tear it in half. Try to squeeze moisture from it; if it's wet or sticky along the tear, continue drying.

Vegetables are dry when there is no moisture left in them. Stalks such as celery and asparagus become brittle sticks, and diced or sliced roots such as carrots, sweet potatoes, and rutabagas become dry, lightweight, woodlike blocks. The consistency of properly dried shredded vegetables might remind you of wood shavings or wood chips.

Dry herbs until they are brittle and crumble easily. Leaves may reach this stage in just a few hours, but stems can take 12 or more hours to dry completely.

Produce Preparation Methods and Drying Times

It's almost meaningless to suggest how long to dry produce. You'll see in the following table that times vary by several hours. Pay the most attention to the smaller numbers: produce rarely dries in less time than the lowest estimate. Check after that amount of time passes, and again every hour or so until the produce is done. Sometimes you'll have to leave things in the dehydrator for many hours past the maximum estimated time.

Drying Mushrooms

You're not supposed to wash mushrooms, so use a soft brush to remove soil. Dry mushrooms whole, or slice ½ inch thick. They'll take 4 to 10 hours to dry, but start on low heat, at about 90 degrees Fahrenheit for 2 hours. Then raise the temperature to 125 degrees until the mushrooms are dried.

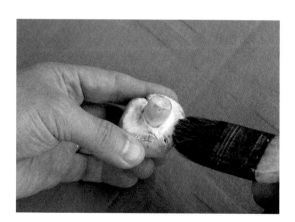

Fruits and Vegetables

along with their methods of preparation and estimated drying times at a temperature between 130 and 140 degrees Fahrenheit.

PRODUCE	PREPARATION	EST. DRYING TIME
Apples	Peel, core, slice ¼–½ inch	4–10 hours
Apricots	Peel (or don't), cut in half, remove pit	8–16 hours
Artichokes	Wash, remove petals, slice hearts an inch wide, blanch	8–12 hours
Asparagus	Wash, cut to desired lengths, blanch	4–12 hours
Bananas	Peel, slice ¼–½ inch	8–12 hours
Beans (green and wax)	Wash, stem, snap to desired lengths, blanch	6–12 hours
Beets	Cook completely, peel, cut ½-inch cubes	4–12 hours
Blueberries	Wash, stem	12–24 hours
Broccoli	Wash, cut into spears, blanch	5–10 hours
Carrots	Peel, slice sticks or ¼–½-inch disks or shred, blanch	6–12 hours
Cauliflower	Wash, cut into spears, blanch	8–16 hours
Celery	Wash, slice ½ inch, blanch	4–10 hours
Cherries	Wash, stem, remove pits	18–26 hours
Corn	Blanch, remove from cob	6–12 hours
Cranberries	Wash, stem, boil until skins crack	10–18 hours
Eggplant	Peel, seed, slice ¼–½ inch, blanch	6–14 hours
Figs	Wash, stem, cut in half	8–16 hours
Grapes	Wash, stem	10–24 hours
Kiwi	Peel, slice ¼–½ inch	6–12 hours
Mangoes	Peel, seed, slice about ½ inch	8–20 hours
Melons	Peel, seed, slice about ½ inch	10–22 hours
Nectarines	Peel (or don't), quarter or slice ½ inch	8–16 hours
Onions	Skin, slice ¼–½ inch or halve, separate layers	6–12 hours
Peaches	Peel, quarter or halve, remove pit	8–16 hours
Pears	Peel, core, slice ¼–½ inch	8–16 hours
Peas	Shell and blanch	5–14 hours
Peppers	Wash, seed, cut as desired	5–12 hours
Pineapple	Peel, core, slice ¼–½ inch	8–14 hours
Plums	Cut in half or quarters, remove pit	8–20 hours
Potatoes	Peel, slice ¼–½ inch, blanch, rinse, dry	10–14 hours
Rhubarb	Wash, cut to 1 inch, steam blanch about 5 minutes	8–14 hours
Strawberries	Wash, stem, halve or slice ½ inch	8–14 hours
Summer squash	Wash, slice ¼–½ inch or shred, blanch	5–10 hours
Sweet potatoes	Peel, slice ¼–½ inch, blanch, rinse, dry	10–14 hours

Dehydration

From the Tip Jar

If your herbs are in flower when you decide to dry them, taste-test them first. Do you notice an off flavor? Bitterness? If they taste bad fresh, they won't taste any better dehydrated.

Restock Your Spice Jars

Cooking in midwinter sometimes makes me long for fresh herbs. When I get a whiff of the dried powders that come from commercial packagers, I sometimes wonder whether those spices really started out as live plants. Amazingly, this isn't the case when I dry my own herbs.

Homegrown and home-dried herbs smell and taste remarkably more like fresh herbs, so stocking your spice cabinet during the growing season can improve the flavors of your cooking year-round.

Herb plants are most flavorful before they mature. Ideally, harvest and dry them before they flower, but don't be timid about drying any herb that you'd be willing to cook with. I harvest cilantro even when the plants contain only thin, fernlike leaves, and I'm never disappointed by the flavor.

Drying Herbs

Harvest as you would when preparing a meal, though for the sake of efficiency, harvest large amounts of herbs to dry all at once. For seeds such as fennel and coriander, leave the seeds attached and harvest the entire seedhead. For small-leafed herbs (such as thyme or rosemary), harvest whole stems and leave the leaves attached.

I always try to fill every tray of my dehydrator before I dry a load of produce. Drying fewer large loads conserves electricity.

Step 2

Rinse the herbs with cold water to remove soil and insects; pick off damaged leaves and stems.

Step 3

Remove whatever water you can—dry the herbs gently with a towel, or spin them for a few turns in a salad spinner.

Step 4

Load the drying trays. Because herbs are thin and lightweight, you can freely overlap stems and leaves as you heap them onto trays. However, even with stems attached, some small-leafed herbs such as thyme may shrink enough as they dry to slip through the holes in the trays. Use a microscreen or a fruit leather pan to contain these small seasonings.

Step 5

Dry herbs at 90 to 100 degrees Fahrenheit until the leaves are crispy and the stems are brittle.

Step 6

Store dried herbs whole in airtight and lightproof containers. Grind them into powder as you need them for cooking, or consider my recommendations below.

When to Powder Herbs

Ideally, store dried herbs as they come out of the dehydrator; don't grind them into powder until you're ready to use them. They'll retain flavor longer. However, for practical purposes it's a lot easier to blend herbs into powder before packaging; they'll require less storage space, you can use them to refill commercial spice jars, and you can grab them off the shelf and put them to use without hassle whenever you need them in recipes. So I encourage you to grind freshly dehydrated herbs and store them in sealed containers in your spice cabinet.

I use a small blender to grind up dried herbs. Don't use a hand blender unless it came with an enclosed container for chopping nuts and other small-volume items. As the blender pulverizes dried herbs, the powder will try to escape.

Herb and Seasoning Preparation Methods and Drying Times

It's almost meaningless to estimate drying times for herbs and other seasonings. Leave things to dry for the shortest time estimated, then check their progress. If your herbs aren't dry, wait another hour or so and check again. Remember that the leaves should crumble easily and the stems should snap clean in half when you bend them.

LEAVES AND STEMS

In all cases, rinse and shake dry before dehydrating.

Herb	Est. Drying Time
Basil	20–24 hours
Chives*	20–24 hours
Mint	20–24 hours
Parsley	20–24 hours
Rosemary	20–24 hours
Sage	20–24 hours
Tarragon	20–24 hours
Cilantro	15–20 hours
Oregano	15–20 hours
Anise	1–3 hours
Dill	1–3 hours
Fennel	1–3 hours
Ginger	1–3 hours
Marjoram	1–3 hours
Thyme	1–3 hours

*Snip chives before dehydrating.

SEEDS

In all cases, estimated drying time is 2 to 5 hours.

Herb	Preparation
Anise	Rinse in cold water, dry
Caraway	Dip seed heads in boiling water, dry
Coriander	Dip seed heads in boiling water, dry
Cumin	Rinse in cold water, dry
Fennel	Rinse in cold water, dry
Mustard	Rinse in cold water, dry

OTHER SEASONINGS

Seasoning	Preparation	Est. Drying Time
Garlic	Peel, slice in half	6–12 hours
Ginger	Rinse, slice ¼–½ inch or grate	2–5 hours
Onions	Peel, slice ¼–½ inch	6–12 hours
Peppers	Wash, slice or dice*	6–12 hours

*For hot pepper seasoning, do not remove seeds or the membranes holding them.

CAUTION!

When you run dried hot chili peppers through a blender to make powder, even a well-sealed blender pitcher might let dust escape. This can be nasty if you inhale it or if it gets in your eyes. (Trust me, I've done it.) Asian cooking sometimes includes crushed dried chili peppers, which are far less hazardous to prepare.

To crush dried peppers, put them in a zipper-top bag, lay the bag on your counter, and work it over with a rolling pin repeatedly until you reduce them to a crumbly collection of seeds and pepper dust.

Air-Dried Herbs

Herbs dry very well in the open air, so you might reduce your electric bill if you reserve the dehydrator for fruits and vegetables. To air-dry herbs, harvest whole branches or even whole plants, and hang them tops-down in a warm, dry place.

Monitor drying herbs for spoilage and be patient. In several days or weeks (depending on the warmth and humidity of your drying space), the leaves and stems of your hanging herbs will become as dry and brittle as if you'd prepared them with an electric food dryer.

Fruit Leathers

You can make leathers (you might know them as "roll-ups") from any fruit, but typically people begin with apples as a base. Apples contain high amounts of pectin, which makes the fruit purée thicken while remaining flexible. Fruits lacking pectin tend to become brittle when they dry, so it's easier to dehydrate apple-based leathers to the right consistency. Apples have a very mild flavor, so when you add other fruits to apple-based leathers, the added fruit flavors tend to dominate.

Step 1

Quarter and core enough apples to fill the pitcher of your blender.

Step 2

Purée the apple quarters until they're smooth; add a bit of water, apple juice, or cider, if necessary, for the right consistency.

Step 3

Place a leather pan on a dehydrator tray and wipe it with a thin coating of vegetable oil.

Step 4

Pour the apple purée into the leather pan. Evenly spread it to a depth of ¼ to ⅜ inch.

Step 5

Dry at 130 to 140 degrees Fahrenheit until the leather is, well, leathery and flexible, but not sticky. This can take 8 or more hours, but check the leathers after 4 hours and monitor them hourly until they're done.

Step 6

Peel the leathers from the pans while they're still warm.

Step 7

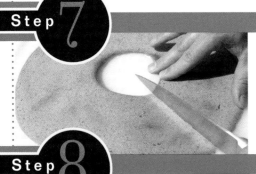

Cut the leathers into serving-sized pieces.

Step 8

Lay each piece of leather on plastic wrap or wax paper, roll up the leather, and wrap. Store in airtight containers.

You can add sugar to the puréed apples if you wish, but high-sugar purée makes drying a bit touchy; leathers with a lot of sugar may become brittle.

Leathers for Grownups

Fruit leathers established themselves in our culture as kids' snack food. Fruity, sweet, and chewy, leathers come in so many colors and flavors. Some even sport drawings you can deform by stretching the leathers before you eat them. (Not that I've ever done that.)

Homemade leathers may lack some of the high-tech appeal of commercially packaged leathers. However, homemade leathers needn't contain the sugar and preservatives that manufacturers add. If that's not enough to sell you on leathers as sophisticated fare, try some of the savory flavor combinations I suggest.

And here's a way to make even fruit-sweet leathers deserving of attention on an hors d'oeuvre plate. Fill your leather pans a bit thin—use only ¼ inch of purée. Store these leathers as usual, but when you want an unusual snack, peel a leather off its plastic sheet and lay a slice of your favorite cheese on it. Then roll the leather together with the cheese on it. If you have only blocks of cheese, cut long rectangular strips and roll them up inside the leathers.

These leather cheese snacks pack dry and won't spoil in a few hours unrefrigerated. So you can send them to school in lunches or pack them as snacks as a nutritious and unexpected alternative to sugary, commercially packaged leathers.

Leathers provide an excellent way to experiment. With puréed apples as a base, add other fruits to the purée to produce different flavors. Or put a thin layer of apple purée in a leather pan, then drizzle strawberry-banana, blueberry, or cherry purée into the apple purée.

For other variations, add spices to the blender as you purée the fruit. One obvious choice is to add cinnamon to puréed apples, strawberries, or cherries. Or add mint leaves when you purée pears. A less obvious combination is pineapple purée with cilantro and cayenne pepper. Take it to a more savory level by adding a bit of onion and tomato as well.

Tomato? Yes, everyone should make tomato leather at least once. Halve the tomatoes and remove the seeds before putting them in the blender. Add fresh basil leaves and a smidge of pepper before blending. Tomato leathers are intensely flavorful and surprisingly sweet. What's more, in a pinch, you can add water and cook tomato leathers to create tomato sauce for pasta dishes.

Cooking with Dehydrated Produce

Dehydrated fruits and vegetables present opportunities to create unique flavor combinations you can't achieve with fresh produce. You might remember the era before sun-dried tomatoes; if anyone was eating these marvels of Italian cooking, they weren't telling the rest of us about it.

Dehydration

Today, you can buy jars of sun-dried tomatoes to pep up pasta dishes, soups, meats, salads, and sauces. Heck, there are even sun-dried tomato salad dressings. What's so great about a sun-dried tomato? Just an awesome tangy tomato explosion in your mouth each time you bite into one! If you haven't eaten a sun-dried tomato straight up, just follow the instructions for creating dehydrated tomato treats in this chapter.

A big part of cooking with dehydrated produce is discovering how to accent meals with the new textures and flavors you create through dehydration. On the other hand, usually you just want good-old regular produce to use in regular old-favorite dishes. Using dried produce decreases the authenticity of such dishes.

Dehydrated Fruit

Dehydrated fruit is a great snack food. Dried blueberries look kind of scary, but the combination of crunchy skins and chewy centers works well when it delivers a concentrated burst of blueberry flavor. The mere idea of dried cantaloupe is bizarre, but crispy chunks are sweet and delicious and could easily replace fatty potato chips in a dieter's snack rotation.

Create your own mixes of dried fruit snacks: apple chips, blueberries, cherries, and strawberries are a great combination, as are pineapple chunks, banana chips, and mango chips. Keep supplies of these snacks at your desk to satisfy your munchies throughout the workday; they're far better for you than candy bars or deep-fried potato chips.

One step removed from simply snacking on dried fruit is including dried fruit in trail mix, snack bars, and baked goods. If you mix your own gorp, toss in handfuls of home-dried raisins, apricots, bananas, or strawberries—whatever you have on hand. In case you've never made gorp—or you don't know what it is—see the instructions in the box "High-Energy Trail Food."

High-Energy Trail Food

I've been a cave explorer and outdoor enthusiast for more than thirty years, and I've made a lot of gorp to take on my expeditions. When I was a kid, gorp was an acronym for Good Old Raisins & Peanuts. It refers to a mixture of foods that you can bag and carry easily for quick snacks when you're hiking or otherwise engaged outdoors. My gorp recipe is rather basic, but delicious. Yield: 6 cups.

2 cups granola cereal or equivalent

1 cup salted, dry-roasted peanuts

1 cup chocolate bits or M&M's

1 cup raisins

1 cup dried apricots or other dried fruit

In a large bowl mix all of the ingredients to distribute them evenly, then package in personal-sized containers.

On long trips, I'll bag a half gallon of gorp to keep with my camping gear. Each day, I'll fill a smaller bag from my stash and carry, perhaps, 2 cups of gorp in my fanny pack.

Rehydrated Fruit? Please, No!

Is your larder full of dehydrated fruits? Are you pining away for a fruit salad? Well, I hope your freezer is full of frozen fruit, or that there's at least one shelf of canned fruit in that crowded larder.

You can rehydrate fruit and use it to create something very like a fruit salad. And if you imagine the worst, you might be surprised at the result: uncooked, rehydrated fruit tastes amazingly like fresh fruit. Unfortunately, it has a most unpleasant texture; it's a bit like a soggy sponge that has soaked up a little slime.

Rehydrated fruit becomes more palatable when you chop it into small pieces and mix it into products such as cottage cheese or yogurt, but even then, you might do better simply to mix in the dried fruit, without rehydrating it.

Rather than rehydrate fruits for salads, use dried fruits for cooked desserts such as cobbler, stewed fruit, and pie filling. Fruits may need to simmer a long time before they resemble their fresh-cooked equivalents.

Dehydration

Fruity Banana Bread

Traditional banana bread recipes often call for chopped nuts. Instead, add dried fruit! Strawberries are popular, but I like pineapple and mango with my bananas. Cherries or blueberries should taste terrific in this bread, and if you like a tart flavor, try using dried rhubarb.

Makes 2 loaves

2 cups dried banana chips or 3 large ripe (or overripe) bananas

1 cup raw sugar (or ½ cup white sugar and ½ cup brown sugar)

2 eggs

1½ sticks butter, melted

2 cups all-purpose flour

2 teaspoons baking soda

3 tablespoons milk soured with ¼ teaspoon vinegar

1 cup bite-sized dried fruit chunks

> ### From the Tip Jar
>
> If you plan to use dried bananas to make banana bread, try making banana powder according to the instructions in "Tricks with Dehydrated Fruit" on page 65.

Bring 3 cups water to a boil in a saucepan, remove it from the heat, and float the banana chips in it for 20 to 40 minutes or until the chips are soft. Pour off any excess water and mash the softened chips in a large bowl (if you're using fresh bananas, don't soak them, just mash them in the bowl).

Preheat the oven to 350 degrees Fahrenheit.

In a large bowl add the sugar and eggs to the mashed bananas and beat until blended. While mixing, drizzle in the melted butter. In a separate bowl stir the baking soda into the flour. Add the flour mixture to the wet ingredients, mixing until the batter is smooth. Stir in the soured milk and fold in the dried fruit chunks.

Grease two 8 x 4-inch loaf pans and divide the batter evenly between them. Bake for 30 minutes at 350 degrees, then lower the temperature to 300 and continue baking another 45 minutes. Remove the loaves from the pans immediately and place on a cooling rack.

Tricks with Dehydrated Fruit

One very cool characteristic of dehydrated food, and I'm talking about food that's bone-dry, is that you can easily reduce it to powder by running it through a blender. For certain fruits, this provides a shortcut to creating sauces and marinades. Try these shortcuts:

Applesauce: Mix one part powdered apples with one part water.

Tomato paste: Mix one part powdered tomatoes with one part water.

Tomato sauce: Mix one part powdered tomatoes and three parts water.

Tomato soup: Mix 1 cup water, 1 cup cream, and about 1 cup tomato powder.

I like to cook Indian food and occasionally I run across recipes that call for mango powder. Of course, I can't find mango powder in local stores, but I can make it easily by grinding dried mango chunks in my blender.

Dry and pulverize bananas and you can create the equivalent of mashed bananas by mixing equal parts banana powder and water.

Fruit powders also make tasty garnishes. Sprinkle powdered cherries, melon, bananas, pineapple, strawberries, or other fruit on puddings, ice cream, cottage cheese, or salad. Mix fruit powders in cream cheese to make fruit spreads for toast and hors

NOTE

I can't emphasize enough that fruits must be very dry before you pulverize them into powder. This means pushing them beyond ideal drying times. Fruit slices that are leathery and flexible will become sticky in a blender, and the resulting powder will form clumps.

d'oeuvres, or mix powders in ricotta to stuff cannoli. Mix fruit powders into cookie dough and cake batter instead of using imitation fruit extracts when you bake.

Dehydrated Vegetables

Dehydrated vegetables generally aren't great snack food. However, they tend to rehydrate far better than fruits do. Some bounce back so well when you add water that you might not be able to distinguish them from fresh, that is, if you cook them. Don't expect to rehydrate dried carrot sticks and snack on them as crudités; even if they absorb water without cooking, they'll come out soggy and droopy.

Use dehydrated vegetables in cooked dishes and you'll have generally decent results. Cooking returns dehydrated vegetables to some semblance of their former selves, and you'll discover that many family favorites come out just fine when you start with dehydrated vegetables.

Dishes that work best with dehydrated vegetables are soups, stews, and casseroles.

Dehydration

Save Time with Dehydrated Aromatic Vegetables

A great way to save time throughout the year is to schedule a few dehydrating days on which you prep and dry aromatic vegetables. The big three aromatic vegetables in cooking, descended from the mirepoix of French cuisine, are onions, celery, and carrots. These vegetables are aromatic (hence the name "aromatics") and form a deep base of flavor.

To dry aromatics, cut them up as you would were you about to cook with them. Blanch the diced carrots and celery. Place microscreen inserts on your dehydrating trays and spread the diced vegetables on the screens. Finally, dry the vegetables for 6 to 12 hours.

Store dehydrated aromatic vegetables in packages appropriate for use in a single dish. The classic mix is two parts onions to one part celery and one part carrots. Or pack large containers of each type of dehydrated aromatic vegetable and combine them as needed throughout the year.

To cook with dehydrated aromatics, follow the recipes as if the vegetables were fresh, decreasing the measured amounts of the aromatics by 50 percent. If the recipe calls for sautéing the aromatics before adding other ingredients, you can add a few tablespoons of water to the pan after browning the dried vegetables; the vegetables will soften as they absorb the water.

Instant Mashed Vegetables?

The title to this section doesn't sound very appetizing, but consider this: mashed potatoes, mashed squash, and mashed sweet potatoes are relatively common fare for people of all ages. Mashed any other type of vegetable is baby food!

You can, of course, cook potatoes and sweet potatoes whole and remove the skins afterward. I prefer to pare the potatoes and cut them into ½-inch slices before cooking. This significantly reduces cooking time and lets me go from cooking to mashing with minimal effort.

NOTE

If you have a bumper crop of potatoes, squash, or sweet potatoes and you don't have a decent cold-storage facility, cook, mash, dry, crumble, and powder your produce. Here's the procedure:

1. Pare and cut up the produce as you would to prepare it for any meal.

2. Fully cook the produce in boiling water.

3. Pour off most of the water (but keep some) and mash the produce. Do not add butter or milk at this point as it can spoil while your produce is in storage. Add water you saved from cooking to thin the mashed produce so it will spread easily in the drying trays.

4. Place a fruit leather pan on a drying tray and add the mashed produce to the pan; spread to an even depth in the pan. If you prefer, add enough water to the mash to make it runny and it will flow easily to fill the leather pan.

5. Dry 4 to 8 hours at 130 to 140 degrees Fahrenheit.

6. Remove the dried mashed produce from the pan and crumble it into small pieces.

7. Grind the crumbled, dried, mashed produce into powder.

8. Store the powdered, crumbled, mashed, dried produce in an airtight container.

To reconstitute the mashed produce, start with ¼ cup powdered material and add it to 1 cup boiling water. Let it sit, covered, for 10 to 20 minutes. Set the mixture on low heat and cook slowly for 10 to 15 minutes. Cook uncovered in the last several minutes to release moisture if the reconstituted produce appears too runny. Add butter, milk, and seasonings as you would to their fresh equivalents. The texture of the rehydrated produce won't match that of fresh, but the flavors will be remarkably similar.

From the Tip Jar

How do you fit 1¼ pounds of potatoes (about 5 to 6 cups diced potatoes) into a 1-cup container? Cook them, mash them, dehydrate them, break them into little pieces, and grind them in a food processor. The resulting "instant mashed potatoes" weigh just 4½ ounces.

More with Potatoes

Potatoes and sweet potatoes are the wunderkinder of vegetable dehydration. Practically anything you cook with fresh potatoes and sweet potatoes you can cook just as well with their dehydrated counterparts. Here are some options to try.

Sliced potatoes and sweet potatoes. Pare the potatoes and slice them into ½-inch segments. Blanch the slices, lay them on drying trays, and dehydrate for 10 to 18 hours. They'll be hard disks when they're dry.

Rehydrate these disks in boiling water until they assume the texture of normally prepared potatoes. After that, fry them in butter, deep fry them, roast them with olive oil and garlic, or candy them (sweet potatoes); in short, treat them like potatoes!

You can leave sliced potatoes dehydrated if you incorporate them into casseroles such as scalloped potatoes or into soups and stews. Add

a bit of extra liquid to the recipe (they'll absorb three to four times their volume in fluid), but otherwise cook as you would raw potatoes.

Diced potatoes. Pare and dice potatoes into ¼- to ⅜-inch cubes. Blanch them and dehydrate them to use for home fries. To rehydrate, boil water, take it off the heat, and add the dehydrated cubes. Usually, the potatoes will bounce back in 20 minutes, but you may need to reheat the water and potatoes to speed rehydration. Once the cubes soften, drain the water and fry the potato cubes in butter with onions, salt, and pepper for classic home fries. Or try my favorite variation, Southwestern Home Fries and Eggs on page 69.

Of course, you can toss handfuls of dried diced potatoes into soups and stews, or use them as a base for casseroles.

Shredded potatoes. Use the shredding face of your grater or the grating disk of your food processor to create heaps of shredded potatoes. Blanch the shreds briefly and dry them on microscreens so they don't fall through the drying trays. Shredded potatoes rehydrate quickly in boiling water. Drain them and use them as if they were fresh to make casseroles, hash browns, or potato soup. Shredded dried potatoes make a great addition to yeast breads and soups; there's no need to rehydrate them before mixing them in.

Southwestern Home Fries and Eggs

This easy-to-make one-skillet breakfast combines traditional country-style fixings with flavors from Mexican cooking. You can make it with dried diced or shredded potatoes or, in a pinch, I suppose you could use fresh potatoes.

Makes 1 serving

½ cup diced dehydrated potatoes or 1 cup shredded dehydrated potatoes

12 slices dried onions or 1 heaping tablespoon dried diced onions

3 strips bacon (optional)

1 to 2 tablespoons butter (if not using bacon)

1 teaspoon dried cilantro

⅛ to ¼ teaspoon ground black pepper (to taste)

⅛ to ¼ teaspoon cayenne pepper (to taste)

Salt to taste

3 eggs

Boil 3 cups water in a saucepan, remove from the heat, and add the dried potatoes and onions. While the potatoes soften, fry the bacon, if using, in a frying pan. Remove the bacon from the pan and reserve for later. Leave the bacon fat in the pan.

When the potatoes are soft (about 20 minutes), heat the bacon fat (or butter) in the frying pan, drain the potatoes and onions, and add them to the frying pan. Fry on medium-high heat, stirring and flipping regularly, until some of the potatoes are golden brown, 5 to 10 minutes.

Season the potatoes with the cilantro, black pepper, cayenne pepper, and salt. Mix the seasonings through, then distribute the potatoes evenly over the bottom of the pan. Lower the heat to medium and crack the eggs onto the potatoes. Add 1 tablespoon water to the pan and cover it with a tight-fitting lid. Check after 3 minutes and remove from the heat when the egg whites are firm but the yolks are still soft. Use a spatula to slide the potatoes and eggs onto a plate and top with the bacon strips.

Tangy Tomato Treats

These simple snacks are curiously all-at-once tangy, sweet, and savory, and they require little effort to create. You'll need a bunch of small to medium-sized fresh tomatoes, a bunch of fresh basil leaves, salt, pepper, onion powder, and, optionally, olive oil. (Don't use olive oil if you plan to store these treats for an extended period; the olive oil could become rancid.)

Here's how to make them:

1. Wash the tomatoes and cut them in half from side to side. Slice larger tomatoes into ½-inch sections, also from side to side.

2. Remove the seeds and the gel that surrounds them.

3. Place the tomato pieces, cut sides up, on a drying tray. If you like, brush them with a liberal coating of olive oil.

4. Sprinkle the tomatoes with salt, pepper, and onion powder.

5. Slice the basil leaves into strips or halves and place one or more pieces on each tomato section. Press the basil firmly against the tomato to help it adhere.

6. Dry the tomatoes for 8 to 12 hours (130 to 140 degrees Fahrenheit). Ideally, remove the tomatoes from the dehydrator before they become crispy. They'll be chewy like raisins.

Mixed Vegetables for Soups, Stews, and Casseroles

So many commercially packaged "meals-in-a-pan" involve pouches of dehydrated vegetables and spices. Typically, you cook fresh meat; add vegetables, spices, and water; and slowly cook it all under a cover until the vegetables are tender. These prepackaged meals are popular because they're easy to prepare, they're ready reasonably quickly, and they taste quite good.

Of course, those commercially packaged meals-in-a-pan contain unneeded salt and other preservatives, and they come in limited flavors (albeit, a whole lot of flavors). When you have a lot of produce to preserve (and the time to spend processing it), put together your own packaged meals-in-a-pan for those future days when you just don't have time to cook from scratch.

On Your Mark! Get Set! Dry!

When space or portability is an issue, no preservation method beats dehydration. For root vegetables and winter squash, dehydration is a decent substitute for cold storage and worth considering if the climate frustrates your design for a root cellar.

For the variety of products you can dehydrate—fruits, fruit leathers, spices, vegetables, soup mixes, backpacking meals, one-skillet dinners—you can quickly recoup the cost of a dedicated food dryer. Still, don't limit yourself to this one method of preserving. Following chapters explore freezing, canning, sugaring, fermenting, and quick pickling—all important for creating a wide selection of food choices during times when local fresh produce isn't in season.

NOTE

Dehydrated one-pan meals are lightweight and compact. They are ideal to carry on backpacking trips. They're also convenient space- and time-savers on camping trips where you'll be cooking meals on a camp stove or in your RV.

Chapter 4

Freezing Fruits and Vegetables

For most produce, no preserving method retains flavors better than freezing does. If it were not for texture changes caused by freezing, the flavors of thawed foods would convince you that they were fresh. Most people are so accustomed to frozen foods that eating home-frozen produce is no change at all.

When you have a dedicated freezer, you have the most convenient automatic food preserver available. In a pinch, you can jam just about anything into your freezer and know it will remain edible days or even weeks later.

Unfortunately, maintaining a store of frozen foods is a higher-risk proposition than keeping foods preserved by other methods. Your freezer could break down, an electrical circuit could fail, or someone could leave the freezer door ajar. In a worst-case scenario, a long-term power outage could lead to a complete meltdown. What's more, should you need to move your food stores, frozen foods present considerable challenges.

From the Tip Jar

If you use a lot of fresh ginger in your cooking (Chinese and Indian dishes often call for it), place a piece of gingerroot in a zipper-top freezer bag and store it in the freezer compartment of your refrigerator. When a recipe calls for ginger, grate what you need from the frozen root and return the rest to your freezer. A piece of gingerroot will stay fresh for months if you keep it frozen.

Freezing Fruits and Vegetables

How Much Can You Save?

When I was a kid, I occasionally heard people insist that it wasn't cost-effective to have a freezer unless you bought whole pigs or half cows, or dozens of chickens in a single transaction. My parents actually did buy sides of beef and whole pigs that we'd cut up and store in a freezer in our basement.

An inexpensive new freezer costs around $500 and should last fifteen years. A freezer uses about $6 of electricity in a month. So to pay for that freezer, you need it to reduce your food costs by an average of $8 to $9 a month or about $103 a year.

If you grow your own fruits and vegetables and preserve them in a freezer, putting up $103 worth each year is a slam dunk. When you buy in bulk you shouldn't find it too challenging to chalk up that much in annual savings.

From the Tip Jar

To help when you make a shopping list, or simply to keep track of what's in your freezer, keep a log in which you note each item you store and check off each item you remove. This may seem excessive, but it's amazing how easily things go "missing" inside a freezer.

Accidental Thaw

Without electricity, a freezer can retain cold temperatures for about twenty-four to forty-eight hours.

Over more than two decades, my deep freezer has experienced three disasters, and one near disaster. What caused the disasters? Twice someone left the freezer door open, which was also the case of the near disaster. (Apparently, it's possible not to learn from experience.) The third disaster occurred when our freezer died of old age.

How do these events become disasters? Sometimes several days pass between our visits to the freezer. If you leave the door open for several days, I promise a lot of stuff is going to thaw.

Dealing with a Thaw

When we found our freezer with the door open, we spent ten or fifteen minutes deciding who to blame. Then, anything that had completely thawed, we tossed—even if it was very cold. Anything that had the least degree of iciness, we agreed hadn't yet spoiled. Anything that was still solidly frozen, we treated as refreezable.

But what to do with all that partially thawed stuff? We cooked! With partly frozen vegetables and meat, we made soup—a vat of soup. Beef roasts and whole chickens we roasted or grilled. Partly thawed fruits we cooked into cheesecakes, sauces, and pies. Then we froze all the cooked stuff and had plenty of ready-to-eat meals on hand.

The Locavore Factor

If you buy produce locally and freeze it, you can use it throughout the off-season, reducing or eliminating your reliance on foods shipped from subtropical and coastal areas, and from the Southern Hemisphere. Shippers must keep produce under refrigeration, so the electricity they use to store produce balances the electricity you use to keep your freezer running. However, because you bought locally grown produce, there is virtually no inherent cost for shipping. That's a significant win for the environment.

Nearly every food keeps well in a freezer, though "well" doesn't mean "perfectly." Freezing causes individual cells in plants and meats to burst. When the food thaws, it tends to lose liquids and end up limp. The effect is most obvious in fruits; vegetables become limp, but they don't necessarily lose liquid.

Unfortunately, problems with freezing don't end there. An electric freezer slows chemical processes in fresh produce, but it can't stop them. Enzymes continue working even when the temperature is well below freezing. The enzyme action is what makes fruits and vegetables ripen and eventually rot.

WARNING!

Don't simply mash vegetables you intend to use as baby food. If any large chunks survive, they could pose a choking hazard. Even processing food in a blender doesn't guarantee you'll eliminate all the chunks. Make baby food by forcing cooked produce through a ricer or a food mill.

Make Your Own Baby Food

There is some excitement about making your own baby food so you can control the ingredients and know that your baby is eating only the highest-quality fare. You'll save time by making and preserving large batches of baby food so you don't have to drag out the necessary gear at every meal. Putting food through a ricer or food mill creates extra steps and extra mess.

Strained fruits can or freeze reliably, so you can use either preservation method to preserve apples, peaches, pears, and other fruits as baby food. Strained vegetables, on the other hand, are not good candidates for canning; the USDA has not determined reliable procedures. However, you can freeze strained vegetables with confidence.

To do this, prepare and fully cook the vegetable. Then put it through a ricer or a food mill to create a smooth, chunk-free mash. Finally, pack the mashed vegetable into serving-sized containers that you can seal with minimal air space around the food. Label the containers with their contents and the date, and freeze.

To stop enzyme action in vegetables, partially cook the vegetables in a process called blanching, which involves heating the vegetables all the way through without softening them significantly. With fruit, you can combat the effects of enzymes by smothering the fruit in sugar and, in some cases, by coating the fruit with a mild acidic solution—lemon juice or ascorbic acid.

The table on page 91 reveals how to prepare fruits and vegetables for freezing. Follow the steps and your fruits and vegetables will keep in the freezer for a year or longer.

Ascorbic Acid

Ascorbic acid is vitamin C. It is most useful in freezing to prevent certain fruits from changing color while they await your attention in your freezer. You can usually find ascorbic acid along with other canning supplies at grocery and department stores. You can also buy ascorbic acid powder at a pharmacy.

To keep fruit from changing color while you're preparing it for the freezer, float it in a solution of 1 teaspoon ascorbic acid dissolved in 1 gallon water. Or float fruit in water treated with ½ to ¾ cups commercially bottled lemon juice per gallon. In either case, drain the fruit before packaging it for your freezer.

Basic Steps for Freezing Fruit

There are 5 steps to freezing fruit, but there are a lot of variations in some of those steps. The U.S. Department of Agriculture publishes best practices, but deviating from those practices isn't life threatening. If you don't follow every procedure, your produce may deteriorate more quickly in your freezer and it may not be appealing to eat, but eating it won't kill you. You can pack fruit plain, in syrup, or in sugar. The procedures for each are quite similar.

Packing in Syrup

NOTE

Fruits and syrups expand as they freeze, so leave ½ to ¾ inch of head space between the lid of a rigid freezer container and the top of whatever you're freezing in it.

Step 1

Prepare the syrup and let it cool. Refer to the "Syrups for Canning Fruit" table on page 132 for specific details. For apples, peaches, apricots, and nectarines, mix ½ teaspoon ascorbic acid with each quart of syrup.

Step 2

Wash, peel, seed, cut up, mash, or otherwise prepare the fruit into shapes you'll use when cooking or serving it later.

Step 3

Package the fruit in freezer bags or freezer containers.

Step 4

Cover the fruit with the sugar syrup.

Peaches in syrup 7/10

Step 5

Seal the containers, label them with the date and contents, and freeze.

 **Step 1**

Wash, peel, seed, cut up, mash, or otherwise prepare the fruit into shapes you'll use when cooking or serving it later.

Step 2

For apples, peaches, apricots, and nectarines, mix ½ teaspoon ascorbic acid with 3 tablespoons water for every quart of prepared fruit. Sprinkle the mixture on the fruit and toss it throughout.

Step 3

Toss the fruit in sugar, distributing the sugar evenly throughout.

Step 4

Package the sugared fruit in freezer bags or freezer containers.

Step 5

Seal the containers, label them with the date and contents, and freeze.

Packing Without Sugar

Step 1
Wash, peel, seed, cut up, mash, or otherwise prepare the fruit into shapes you'll use when cooking or serving it later.

Step 2
For apples, peaches, apricots, and nectarines, mix ½ teaspoon ascorbic acid with 3 tablespoons water for every quart of prepared fruit. Sprinkle the mixture on the fruit and toss it throughout.

Step 3
Package the fruit in freezer bags or freezer containers.

Basic Steps for Freezing Vegetables

Step 1

Wash, pare, and cut the vegetables into shapes you'll use when cooking them later.

Step 2

Blanch the vegetables. Refer to "How to Blanch" on page 87 for specifics about blanching vegetables.

Step 3

Pack the vegetables into zipper-top freezer bags or into other resealable freezer containers.

Step 4

Label each container with a description of its contents and the date, and then freeze.

Say No to Frozen Lumps

When you're freezing fruits or vegetables, you face the challenge of the ages: if you pack a bunch of damp vegetable pieces into a bag or box and freeze them, you end up with a large, frozen lump of vegetables. This isn't a huge problem if you anticipate it and package no more in a container than you'll consume in a single use.

From the Tip Jar

If you fill a half dozen or so 1-cup packages with fruits or vegetables, keep them organized by putting those packages inside a larger container. This way you won't have to dig through the freezer looking for all those smaller bags or containers.

A single serving of vegetables might be ¼ to ½ cup. So for a family of four, pack about 1 to 2 cups of vegetables per freezer bag or container. When it's time to serve, dump them into a saucepan or microwave-safe bowl and the lump will thaw out as it heats.

Processing foods into single-meal portions for storage takes a bit of work. What's more, it limits the usability of the produce later on. Suppose, for example, that you're preparing a vegetable-heavy stir-fry and all your vegetables come out of the freezer in lumps. You'll need to thaw the vegetables to some degree before you add them to your frying pan or wok. And forget those days when your family is away and you need only enough vegetables for one person; you'll need an ice pick to hack a smaller lump of vegetables away from the lump you froze to feed your family.

Individually Frozen Fruits and Vegetables

You can eliminate the hassle of dealing with frozen lumps if you're willing to change things up a bit when you process produce for freezing. Instead of packing fruits and vegetables directly into freezer containers or freezer bags, spread them one layer deep on jellyroll or pizza pans, then slide them into your freezer until the produce freezes. I usually have two or three pans to freeze at once, and I leave them overnight.

Freezing Fruits and Vegetables

Later, remove the pans from the freezer, flex them to loosen the frozen produce, and transfer the produce into freezer containers or bags. Work quickly so the produce doesn't thaw. After labeling the containers, return them to the freezer.

Using this approach, you can pack 1- or 2-gallon containers with produce and easily remove only what you want to use when you're ready to cook with it.

How to Blanch

The USDA recommends two methods of blanching vegetables: boiling water blanching and steam blanching. For both methods, prepare the vegetables as you would if you were about to cook them—shell them, peel them, skin them, remove the seeds, and cut them into pieces if that's how you like them. For more specific guidelines, refer to "Produce-Specific Procedures" (page 187) in Chapter 7. For each type of vegetable listed there, you'll find the subheads "Select" and "Prepare" with information about readying vegetables for preservation.

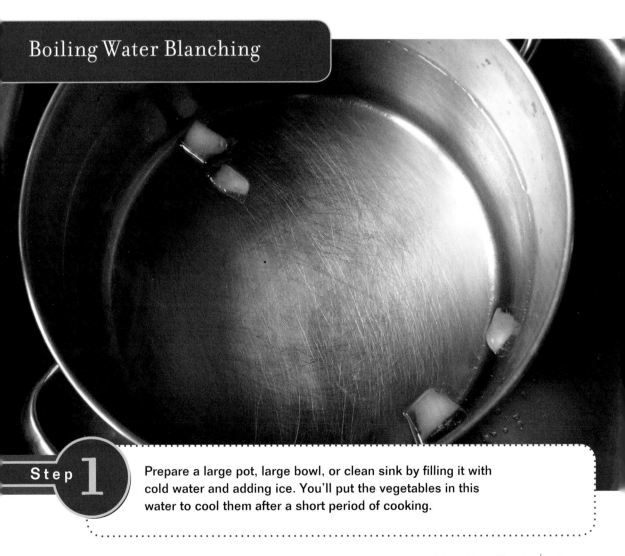

Boiling Water Blanching

Step 1 Prepare a large pot, large bowl, or clean sink by filling it with cold water and adding ice. You'll put the vegetables in this water to cool them after a short period of cooking.

Step 2

Fill a large pot with hot water and heat it to a boil. Ideally, use a pot that has a removable strainer such as a pasta cooker. Barring that, you'll need a strainer that can fit inside the pot you use.

Step 3

Fill the strainer about halfway with prepared vegetables and lower it into the boiling water (if you pack in the vegetables, you'll wait a long time for the water to return to boiling). As soon as the water resumes boiling, time the cooking for the number of minutes listed in the "Blanching Times" table on page 91.

Step 4

At the end of the specified cooking time, immediately remove the strainer holding the vegetables from the boiling water and plunge the strainer into the ice water; let the vegetables cool for the same number of minutes they cooked.

Step 5

Remove the vegetables from the ice water bath and drain them on a towel. Blot the vegetables to remove as much moisture as possible before packing them into freezer containers.

Steam Blanching

Step 1

Prepare a large pot, large bowl, or clean sink by filling it with cold water and adding ice. You'll put the vegetables in this water to cool them after a short period of cooking.

Step 2

For steam blanching, you need a cooking pot that has a basket strainer and a lid. Put about 2 inches of water in the pot, install the basket strainer insert, and heat to a boil.

Step 3

When the water is boiling, fill the basket strainer with prepared vegetables and put the lid on the pot. Start timing immediately and cook for the number of minutes listed in the "Blanching Times" table on page 91.

Step 4

When the time is up, remove the basket strainer from the pot and plunge it into the ice water (or dump the vegetables into the ice water if the basket strainer doesn't fit). Let the vegetables cool about half of the time they were in the steamer.

Step 5

Remove the vegetables from the ice water bath and drain them on a towel. Blot the vegetables to remove as much moisture as possible before packing them into freezer containers.

BLANCHING TIMES

The time ranges indicate less processing time for smaller vegetables and more processing time for larger vegetables.

PRODUCE	BOILING TIME	STEAMING TIME
Asparagus	2–4 minutes	3–6 minutes
Beans (green, snap, string, wax)	3 minutes	4½ minutes
Beets	Cook fully	n/a
Broccoli	3 minutes	5 minutes
Brussels sprouts	3–5 minutes	4½–7½ minutes
Cabbage, shredded	1½ minutes	3 minutes
Carrots	2–5 minutes	3–7½ minutes
Cauliflower	3 minutes	4½ minutes
Celery	3 minutes	4½ minutes
Corn on the cob	7–11 minutes	10–16 minutes
Corn (remove from cob after blanching)	4 minutes	6 minutes
Eggplant	4 minutes	6 minutes
Greens (collards)	3 minutes	4½ minutes
Greens (other than collards)	2 minutes	3 minutes
Lima beans	2–4 minutes	3–6 minutes
Okra	3–4 minutes	4½–6 minutes
Onions (whole)	3–7 minutes	4½–11 minutes
Peas (shelled)	1½ minutes	3 minutes
Peas (snow peas)	1½–3 minutes	2½–4½ minutes
Peppers, bell	2–3 minutes	3–4½ minutes
Summer squash	3 minutes	4½ minutes
Winter squash and pumpkins	Cook fully	n/a

Freezing Fruits and Vegetables

Homemade Frozen Dinners

With freezing, consider the meaning of the word "fresh." We typically eat fruit raw, so freezing it and thawing it robs it of characteristics we think of as fresh. We typically cook vegetables before eating. So if your thawed vegetables cook up as if they're fresh, you've done pretty well.

Here's the special advantage of freezing: once you cook something—nearly anything—it freezes and thaws very convincingly. If you can't think of a preservation method to do a satisfactory job for a specific fruit or vegetable, cook the produce into whatever dish you'd use it in anyway, then freeze the prepared dish.

Eggplant may be the poster child for this idea. Eggplant gets so mushy when you cook it that freezing and thawing it first doesn't do it any favors. However, if you cook eggplant into a pasta dish, moussaka, or eggplant parmigiana, you can freeze it for long-term storage and serve it with confidence.

It's nearly impossible to thaw a meal so the vegetables are crisp. But when ingredients are inexpensive, you can save by cooking up extras of your favorite dishes and freezing portions for meals later in the year.

NOTE

For several years, I've cooked Thanksgiving dinner for my family at my dad's house. There's always plenty left over, which I package into individual meals: I use snack-sized zipper-top bags and fill each one with a one-person serving of turkey, mashed potatoes and gravy, stuffing, sweet potatoes, bean casserole, or corn pudding.

To make a meal, I collect one bag of each type of food and put them together in a single freezer bag. If everything divides equally, I usually have eight to ten freezer bags, each filled with the six individual bags of the turkey and fixings. I put these in my dad's freezer, and he has many chances to enjoy Thanksgiving dinner later.

Due to concerns about toxic chemicals that may escape from hot plastic, I encourage my dad not to reheat his Thanksgiving leftovers in the plastic zipper-top bags. I tell him to empty them onto a plate, cover the plate with a second plate (face down), and heat the meal in his microwave oven.

Fresh Fruit Pies in Any Season

In temperate climates fruits have their seasons. We see rhubarb in mid-spring, followed by strawberries, then raspberries and cherries, peaches and blueberries, and finally pears and apples. Okay, there are blackberries, currants, loganberries, mulberries, plums, and figs as well.

The truth in all this is that each fruit has a limited season. I can buy locally grown strawberries for four to six weeks starting in June. Local sour cherries are usually available for two or three weeks, but I've never seen sour cherries shipped in from out of the area.

To get full enjoyment out of the various fruit seasons, I gorge on whatever's available locally. One of my favorite fruit treats is pie. If you've never made a pie, please hang tight and learn to do so. Most folks seem impressed when you serve a fresh fruit pie, and cooking it is quite easy. Better still, fruit pies keep astonishingly well in a freezer; you can make and freeze extra pies during fruit season, and they'll taste fresh when you bake them in midwinter.

TO MAKE PIE CRUST, YOU'LL NEED THE FOLLOWING INGREDIENTS AND SUPPLIES:

1. 2 cups flour
2. 1 teaspoon salt
3. ½ cup vegetable oil (I prefer to use canola oil)
4. 5 tablespoons milk
5. Wax paper
6. Rolling pin

To make a fruit filling, you'll need about 4 cups fruit (for a 9-inch pie), 1 to 2 cups sugar, and up to ½ cup flour.

CAN TOO! Extra

A 9-inch pie pan can hold about 3 cups of fruit to about 5 cups, depending on how deep the pan is. To ensure that I prepare the right amount of fruit, I fill an empty pie pan with the fruit as I prepare it. When the pan is full, I dump the fruit into a bowl where I'll mix it with sugar and flour later.

Steps to Making and Freezing a Fruit Pie

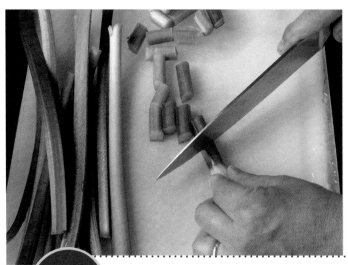

Step 1

Wash, peel, core, pit, cut up, and otherwise prepare the fruit into bite-sized pieces. Place the fruit in a large bowl. In this example, I am preparing a strawberry and rhubarb filling, but the method applies for any basic fruit pie.

Step 2

Measure the flour into a separate medium-sized bowl and stir in the salt.

Step 3

Combine the oil and milk in a separate small bowl. Don't mix these; the milk will settle to the bottom of the container.

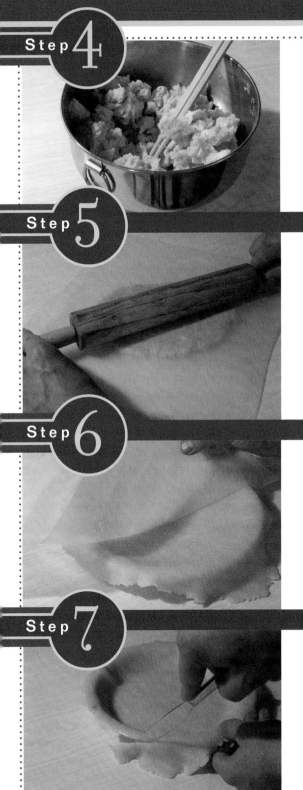

Step 4

Pour the oil and milk into the flour and salt, and stir until the dry stuff has absorbed the wet stuff; don't overmix. Use your hands to pack the dough into a ball.

Step 5

Tear the dough ball in half, press half of it into a disk, and place the disk on a piece of wax paper. Cover it with a second sheet of wax paper and roll it into a perfect 12-inch circle. (Okay, get it kind of round.) To measure, place an empty pie pan upside down on the dough; when the dough sticks out about 1 to 1½ inches all the way around, you've rolled it out enough.

Step 6

Use the flattened dough to line a pie pan. Push the dough down along the sides of the pan so it's in direct contact with the pan throughout.

Step 7

Trim the excess dough around the edge of the pan, leaving the dough flush with the outer edge.

Step 8

Mix the sugar and flour in a small bowl and pour the mixture onto the prepared fruit. (See the "How Much Sugar in Your Pie?" box on page 98 for instructions on sweetening a fruit pie.) Toss the fruit to coat it thoroughly with the sugar and flour.

Step 9

Dump the fruit mixture into the prepared pie pan and distribute it evenly. Don't omit any sugar. Sometimes it won't all adhere to the fruit, so sprinkle or mound it evenly on top of the fruit in the pie crust.

Step 10

Roll out the second ball of dough, and use a pizza cutter or table knife to cut the dough into ¾-inch strips.

Step 11

Lay the dough strips on the pie to create a lattice-style grid.

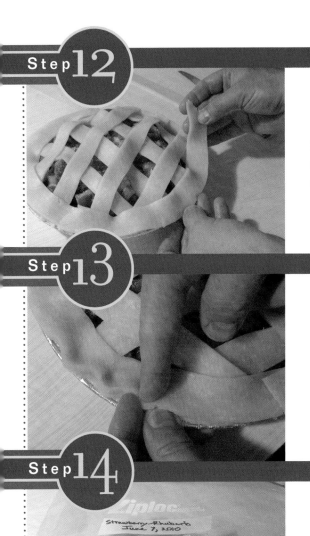

Step 12

Lay more dough strips around the edge of the pie, covering the ends of the dough strips that make up the lattice.

Step 13

Pinch the dough to create a fluted edge all the way around the pan.

Step 14

Insert the pie into a 2-gallon zipper-top freezer bag, mark the bag with the type of pie and the date you created it, and find a level spot for it in the freezer.

Freezing Fruits and Vegetables

How Much Sugar in Your Pie?

For a fruit pie to hold together, you need to add sugar and a thickener to the fruit before cooking. Thickeners include flour, cornstarch, tapioca, custard, and Clear Jel (a modified cornstarch recommended by the USDA to thicken foods for canning). Except on rare occasions, I thicken my fruit pies with flour.

The apple pie is the baseline from which I judge the sweetening and thickening of all fruit pies. It has always stuck in my mind that it takes 1 cup sugar and 3 tablespoons flour to sweeten and thicken an apple pie. After that, I consider a fruit's juice content and natural tartness, and come up with an appropriate mix of sugar and flour.

From the Tip Jar

If you don't use enough flour to thicken your fruit pie filling, the pie will be runny, but it will still taste good. If you use too much flour, the filling may set up and you'll taste the flour.

Here are general guidelines for some of the more common fruits and fruit combinations; you'll have to experiment to find combinations that suit your tastes.

FRUIT	SUGAR	FLOUR
Apple	1 cup	3 tablespoons
Blueberry	1 cup	3 tablespoons
Cherry (sour)	1½ cups	½ cup
Cherry (sweet)	1 cup	⅓ cup
Peach	1 cup	¼ cup
Peach-blueberry	1 cup	5 tablespoons
Pineapple	1 cup	¼ cup
Pineapple-blueberry	1 cup	5 tablespoons
Rhubarb	1½ cups	3 tablespoons
Strawberry-rhubarb	1¼ cups	⅓ cup

How to Cook a Frozen Pie

When you're ready for a peak-season fresh fruit pie in winter, preheat the oven to 325 degrees Fahrenheit. Put the frozen pie on a pizza pan (line the pan with aluminum foil for easy cleanup later) and bake it for about 30 minutes. Then increase the oven temperature to 400 degrees and continue baking for another 30 to 45 minutes.

I continue baking a fruit pie until the juice in the middle of it bubbles, unless the crust is becoming alarmingly dark. If your crust darkens before the center of the pie bubbles, try finishing the pie at 375 degrees rather than 400.

Fresh (or frozen) fruit pies are excellent à la mode, with whipped cream, or "neat."

Cooking with Frozen Produce

There should be little mystery about using frozen produce in your cooking. In fact, many modern recipes specify frozen ingredients or provide alternative instructions in case you must rely on frozen. Here are a few notes to help in case you're not familiar with the subtleties of frozen produce.

Vegetables. When cooking frozen vegetables, be aware that they're already partially cooked and that freezing has softened them. If you're going to serve them plain, cook them lightly. When I cook homegrown frozen wax beans or peas, I add them to a pot of hot tap water and bring the water to a boil. At most, I leave the pot boiling for a minute before I remove it from the heat and drain the vegetables.

Freezing Fruits and Vegetables

Garden-Fresh Herbs Year-Round

No one complains when you use dried herbs to season foods. But cooking with fresh herbs lifts many dishes to beyond the ordinary. Fresh basil, oregano, thyme, and rosemary make pizza and spaghetti sauce extraordinary, and fresh cilantro imbues many Indian and Mexican dishes with unique flavor.

If you grow your own herbs, you can preserve them in your freezer to provide that fresh herb taste even when your garden is buried in snow. Here's how:

1. Harvest, rinse, and prepare a large quantity of the herb you wish to preserve. By "prepare" I mean separate leaves from stems, or seeds from stalks, as you would when using the herb in cooking.

2. Purée the prepared herb in your blender along with a few tablespoons of water. The goal is to produce a slurry.

3. Fill ice cube trays with the herb slurry and freeze them until they're solid.

4. Pop the herb ice cubes from the trays, load them into freezer containers or zipper-top freezer bags, label them, and return them to the freezer.

From the Tip Jar

If you buy fresh herbs at the grocery store and use only part of the package, preserve the rest with this technique and you'll cut your expenses the next time you need that particular herb.

If you prefer to steam vegetables, check for doneness after about half of the cooking time you use for fresh vegetables. Remove the vegetables from the steamer when they appeal to your sensibilities, and note the total cooking time. I can't provide specifics because freezer temperatures can vary; it takes longer to steam vegetables that start out at 24 degrees Fahrenheit than it does to cook vegetables that start at 32 degrees.

NOTE

If you have an abundance of onions you wish to preserve, dice them, blanch them, and spread them on pizza pans for freezing. With a few gallons of individually frozen onion bits on hand, you'll save a lot of prep time for future recipes that call for diced onion.

To use frozen vegetables in stir-fry dishes (or to sauté them), add the vegetables directly from the freezer to the wok (or frying pan).

Fruit. Cooking with frozen fruit is not very different from cooking with fresh fruit: for most applications you can add the frozen items to a marinade, a dressing, a pot, a frying pan, or a roasting pan and things will work out quite nicely. Of course, using frozen fruit may extend the cooking time a bit. For a fine discussion about adjusting your cooking methods for frozen fruits, please read "Blueberry Pancakes: His and Hers."

Blueberry Pancakes: His and Hers

I freeze about 2 gallons of blueberries each July, which is peak blueberry season in central Pennsylvania. My family goes to a "u-pick" berry farm and returns with 25 to 30 pounds of hand-picked fruit (which is about 25 to 30 quarts of berries). Many of the berries end up in pies, but we love having a bunch of individually frozen blueberries to get us through the rest of the year.

How do we use frozen blueberries? Pancakes.

His pancakes: Normally, I cook pancakes at a medium-high temperature: 6 on a stove knob that tops out at 9. When I put frozen blueberries in the pancakes, I turn the temperature under the skillet to medium, about 4½ out of 9. The pancakes cook slowly, giving the blueberries time to thaw and the batter around them time to cook completely.

Her pancakes: When my wife makes pancakes, she takes a cup or so of blueberries out of the freezer and lets them sit in a bowl for twenty or more minutes before she cooks the pancakes. When she spoons batter into the pan, the blueberries are half-thawed and a bit mushy. Even with the skillet at a medium-high temperature, the pancake batter cooks all the way through.

Freezing Fruits and Vegetables

Freeze ½-cup servings of your favorite fruits rolled or shaken in sugar. In the dog days of summer, chow down as the fruit begins to thaw. The sweet, half-frozen treats are a delicious, refreshing snack.

Down a Slippery Slope

Learning to freeze freshly harvested, locally grown produce can be amazingly satisfying. A freezer full of fruits, vegetables, herbs, desserts, and frozen dinners will feed your family throughout the year.

My wife has explained to me repeatedly how I should thaw the blueberries before I use them, but I never seem to learn. On the other hand, my wife has never rejected one of my slow-cooked blueberry pancakes.

For the most part, people freeze fruit intending to consume it raw rather than cooked. Because the fruit will lose moisture and become mushy when it thaws, it's usually most appealing to eat while it's partially frozen. So, add fully frozen fruit to fruit salad just before you serve it.

In the event you've never had the best fruit salad ever, check out "Mom Used Frozen Fruit in the Best Fruit Salad Ever" on page 103.

But don't stop with freezing. Learn to can both high-acid and low-acid foods as explained in upcoming chapters. In time, you'll develop preferences for which foods you put up using each of the preservation methods you master. You might guess from this chapter that fruit pies occupy a lot of space in my freezer; I prefer to assemble the pies and freeze them rather than to can pie filling and use it to make pies later.

I tend to freeze vegetables such as beans, peas, and winter squash, and I freeze various types of berries. However, I would rather can jams and jellies than make the freezer versions, and I find tomato and applesauce far more convenient canned than frozen.

In Chapter 5, you'll learn how to can high-acid foods such as fruit (including tomatoes), pickles, and relishes. Actually, Chapter 5 focuses on fruit and the fundamental procedures of canning. Later chapters use the skills you learn in Chapter 5 to preserve jams, jellies, fermented vegetables, quick pickles, and relishes.

Mom Used Frozen Fruit in the Best Fruit Salad Ever

Frozen fruit in the best fruit salad ever? A travesty? No, it's a benefit of preserving fruits by freezing them. Mom made this salad again and again when grapefruit was in season—which happened to be during winter in upstate New York. Few pleasures in life are as easy to create as this masterpiece of culinary artistry. These instructions make enough salad to serve five or six people.

2 fresh grapefruits

2 fresh bananas

Sugar to taste

1 cup frozen strawberries

1 cup frozen blueberries

1. *Wash the grapefruits, halve them, seed them, and use a teaspoon to dig the segments out of the halves. Work over the serving bowl so all the fruit and juice end up in it.*

2. *Peel the bananas and slice them into the serving bowl.*

3. *Add sugar to taste; mix it in so it dissolves completely.*

4. *Minutes before serving, add the frozen strawberries and blueberries to the serving bowl and mix them thoroughly.*

Warn your guests that some of the fruit might still be frozen.

Chapter 5

Canning High-Acid Foods
No Special Equipment Required

As good as commercially canned fruits may taste, there are amazing differences between the flavors and textures of store-bought canned fruits and home-canned fruits.

Every time I serve home-canned applesauce, I marvel at how the first spoonful tastes remarkably like freshly cooked applesauce; I've never had that experience eating commercially canned applesauce. Home-canned peaches, pears, and pineapples taste sweet and fruity— certainly not like fresh fruit, but far more natural than commercially canned fruit.

Canned fruit offers amazing convenience— vitamin-rich, delicious foods that keep for years without refrigeration. My mom mixed canned fruit into flavored gelatin, served it over cottage cheese, stirred it into yogurt, and cooked it into main courses and desserts. She got no complaints from her family about canned fruit.

After frozen fruit, home-canned fruit is closer to fresh fruit in flavor and texture than any other preserved fruit. Canning, unfortunately, cooks the fruit. On the other hand, once canned, fruit will keep for six

months to a year without refrigeration. That's a considerable advantage in the event of lengthy power outages or the accidental defrosting of your freezer. What's more, it costs nothing to store canned goods at room temperature; to cover the expense of operating a freezer, you need to realize cost savings with the produce you preserve.

Canning High-Acid Foods

How Canning Preserves Food

Canning involves packaging produce in glass jars, putting special lids on the jars, and cooking them for specific periods of time. Folks at the United States Department of Agriculture have tested extensively, and they publish cooking times that ensure reliable preservation.

Canning kills germs. Fruits and vegetables harbor microorganisms that won't harm you if you eat them raw or freshly cooked. The worst of these microbes, Clostridium botulinum, exists as harmless spores on virtually all fresh fruits and vegetables. However, when you submerge botulinum spores in water and deprive them of oxygen, they "hatch" into active bacteria and produce botulinum toxin. Even tiny amounts of botulism can kill a person, so it's important to destroy all the botulinum spores on canned foods.

To kill these nasty spores in the absence of acid, you must cook them at 240 degrees Fahrenheit or hotter for lengths of time determined by the type of food you're preserving. The acid in high-acid foods contributes to killing botulinum spores, so the 212 degrees Fahrenheit temperature of boiling water is sufficient.

To assure there is enough acid to sterilize your produce, some canning recipes call for added lemon juice, vinegar, ascorbic acid (vitamin C), or citric acid. Pickling, in fact, relies on the acid in vinegar to fend off microbes from produce that otherwise lacks sufficient acid for the feat. Proper canning destroys molds, yeasts, and other microbes along with the botulinum spores.

Canning stops enzymes. Naturally occurring enzymes in food actually cause food to spoil. Refrigeration slows these enzymes, extending the life of produce for several days or weeks. Canning destroys the enzymes so they no longer cause food to deteriorate.

Canning captures nutrients. Vitamins in foods deteriorate over time. After a day or two at room temperature, vegetables may lose half of the vitamins they had at harvest. Ideally, you can vegetables and fruits on the day you harvest them. And while canning reduces some vitamins, notably vitamins A, C, thiamin, and riboflavin, it preserves other vitamins quite well. Food you can on the day of harvest quite likely contains more vitamins per pound than fresh produce you buy in a grocery store.

Canning eliminates oxygen. Food in contact with air deteriorates through oxidation. The food's color, texture, and flavor change, and it becomes less palatable. Canning forces air out of the canning jars and establishes a vacuum that keeps the lid on the jar and keeps food from oxidizing.

More about Acidity

The USDA identifies two categories of foods relevant to canning: high-acid and low-acid. All fruits (including tomatoes) are in the high-acid category, while vegetables and meats are low-acid foods.

This distinction matters because you preserve high-acid foods by canning them at the temperature of boiling water. To preserve low-acid foods, you need to use a pressure canner that can raise the temperature to 240 degrees Fahrenheit—well above the boiling point of water.

Canning high-acid foods is surprisingly easy. In fact, most of the work involves simply cleaning, paring, pitting, and cutting the fruits you wish to preserve. Once you've made a vat of applesauce, it's not a whole lot of work to pack it in jars and cook them in a boiling water bath canner.

There's more good news about canning high-acid foods: other than canning jars, lids, and bands, you need no special equipment. You can process produce in any pot that's at least 1½ inches taller than your canning jars. There are, however, some specialized pieces of equipment that simplify boiling water bath canning. They're not expensive and they last as many years as you're likely to use them, so this basic gear is a worthwhile investment.

Candidates for Boiling Water Bath Canning

All fruits (including tomatoes) and fruit juices
....

Pickles (pickled vegetables)
....

Fermented vegetables
....

Relishes and some chutneys
....

Jams, jellies, and preserves
....

Syrups
....

A boiling water bath canner can process only high-acid foods. A pressure canner (right) can process both low-acid and high-acid foods.

Canning High-Acid Foods

Necessary Equipment for Canning

To prepare foods for canning, you need paring and cutting knives, measuring cups and spoons, bowls, and saucepans, all of which you almost certainly own if you have even a modestly equipped kitchen.

The list of specialized equipment you must have for home canning is short.

Canning jars. Use only jars specifically made for home canning. Lids and bands may fit on jars that originally were full of mayonnaise, jelly, or pickles, but commercial canners don't use jars intended for repeated boiling and cooling. You can find home canning jars at department, grocery, and hardware stores during canning season. Many suppliers sell home canning equipment year-round on the Internet. Canning jars usually come with lids and bands, so you don't need to buy those separately until you're ready to refill jars you've already used.

Canning lids. A lid is a nearly flat metal disk with a ring of sealant on one side. Sealants differ depending on the manufacturer, so review the literature that comes with the lids or the canning jars. *Use a canning lid only one time!* Cooking and cooling the lid on a canning jar redistributes the sealant so it's likely to perform badly if you use it again.

Canning bands. A band is a threaded ring of metal that screws onto the threads of a canning jar and holds a lid against the jar's rim. You can reuse bands until they rust badly or they bend out of shape.

Deep pot. Any pot will do as long as it's 1½ inches deeper than the tallest canning jar you want to process. You need to submerge the jars 1 inch or more beneath the surface of the boiling water, and it's useful to place something under them so they don't clatter against the bottom while cooking. Of course, the bigger the diameter of your pot, the more jars you can fit in it. A typical canning pot holds seven 1-quart jars or, perhaps, nine 1-pint jars (no stacking allowed).

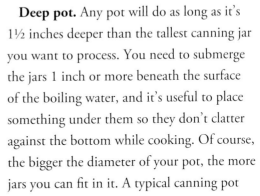

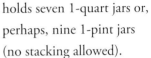

The home canning industry has developed other specialized equipment that simplifies some canning tasks. You may want to do a small-batch canning project to evaluate your enthusiasm for canning before you invest in all the gear. Once you commit to canning as part of your food-preserving strategy, the following items will help streamline your canning activities.

Dedicated canning pot and jar rack. A canning pot should come with a rack. For boiling water bath canners, the rack typically has handles that let you suspend it only partially submerged in the pot. You can use the handles to lower the jars to the bottom of the pot and to lift them back up.

Canning High-Acid Foods

Jar lifter. I'd hate to process canned goods without a jar lifter. A jar lifter is like huge pliers you use to grab a jar by the neck and either place it into the boiling water bath, or remove it from the boiling water.

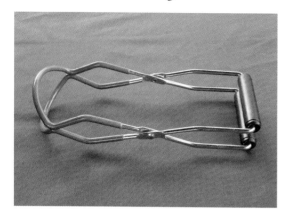

Canning funnel. A canning funnel has a wide opening at the bottom that fits easily into the mouth of a standard canning jar. The top of the funnel is quite a bit wider so you can easily slide produce down the sides of the funnel into a jar, or pour hot liquids or sauces into the jar without splashing on the jar's lip. Using a canning funnel makes packing the jars significantly easier.

The following items are also available, but only marginally more useful than other kitchen implements.

Lid lifter. This is no more than a magnet mounted on the end of a stick. With it, you can easily fish a lid or a band out of a pot of hot water without burning your fingers. You can use tongs for this task instead, but trust me when I say you'll like the lid lifter.

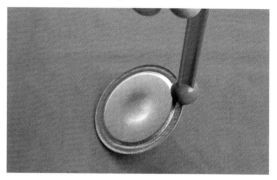

Band tightener (or lid wrench). A band tightener looks like an oversized nutcracker. You can use one to get extra leverage when tightening a band onto a canning jar. Most folks are strong enough to tighten bands by hand. I use a potholder or a dishtowel to handle a hot jar while I screw the band on and tighten it down.

Bubble releaser. Manufacturers make plastic sticks you can use to release air bubbles trapped by produce in a newly filled canning jar. I use a chopstick. One big advantage to the chopstick: I have at least a dozen in my kitchen so I can always find one. Were

I to buy a dedicated bubble-releasing plastic stick, I'd never be able to find it on canning day. You could use a rubber spatula or a wooden skewer, but don't use a knife or any other utensil made of metal or ceramic.

Ladle. While you might use a ladle to spoon syrups, sauces, jams, and jellies into canning jars, I recommend instead that you get a stainless steel 1-cup measuring cup with a handle. The measuring cup is easy to maneuver in tight spaces, and it can fill a quart-sized jar in five or six scoops.

You can buy each specialized canning item individually, but manufacturers also sell them in sets that offer significantly better values. For example, buying a canning funnel and jar lifter individually can cost as much as buying a kit that includes a funnel and jar lifter as well as tongs, a lid lifter, and a lid wrench.

A complete boiling water bath canning set will include a canning pot, a jar rack, a canning funnel, a jar lifter, an instruction manual, and probably a lid lifter and bubble releaser. It might also include enough canning jars, lids, and bands to preserve a single batch of produce.

Before You Buy a Canning Pot

How serious are you about canning? For many, boiling water bath canning is the gateway drug that leads to quick pickling, hard-core pressure canning, and even vegetable fermentation. Unless you rely on quick pickling or fermentation, you'll need a pressure canner to preserve vegetables through canning. Don't jump right into pressure canning; processing several batches of high-acid foods in a boiling water bath canner provides great experience that's helpful as you learn pressure canning.

That said, you should consider buying a pressure canner as your first canning pot. You can use the pressure canner for boiling water bath canning without ever locking the lid and cooking under pressure. An inexpensive pressure canner is three to five times the cost of an inexpensive boiling water bath canner; if you forego the boiling water bath canner, you can apply that initial investment toward the bigger habit you're likely to develop. Having only the pressure canner means you have one fewer (large) pots to store.

If you don't want to commit to a pressure canner, evaluate the pots you already own: could you stand three, five, or seven quart jars in one of them and add enough water so that the jars are 1½ inches below the surface? You may be able to find an inexpensive canning rack to fit your pot. A canning rack holds the jars off the bottom of the pot so they don't bang around too much while they're cooking.

Basic Steps for Boiling Water Bath Canning

There are fifteen steps to boiling water bath canning. Follow these for every batch, varying only the amount of time the filled jars cook in the canner according to the table on page 118. Here's how to proceed:

Step 1

Prepare the produce. You'll find instructions for preparing many types of produce on pages 119 and 187.

Step 2

Inspect the canning jars for cracks or chips—particularly around the rims. Discard any damaged jars. Don't take chances.

Step 3

Wash the jars—even if they are brand-new—and keep them as hot as you can until you're ready to fill them (see the box "Boil Jars to Save Effort" on page 117).

It seems cost-effective to me to put my empty jars in the canner while it's heating. The jars heat up gradually and, if I let them boil for ten minutes, they're sterile when I'm ready to use them. If you do this, manage the water carefully.

Step 4

Place the canning lids into a saucepan or pot, cover them with hot water, and set them on the stove to heat. In most cases, you should not boil the lids, but just keep them very hot. Check the literature packed with the lids for specifics about heating and holding.

You don't need to heat the bands and keep them that way before applying them. However, since I already keep the lids near boiling, I toss in the bands as well so I can find them easily when I'm filling jars.

Step 5

Fill the canning pot with water to within an inch of the top if your empty jars are in it. Otherwise, fill the pot just over half full. Cover the pot and set the dial to high heat until the water is boiling.

Step 6

Fill the hot canning jars according to the instructions for the produce you're canning. For sauces and syrups, this will involve filling the hot jars with hot produce. For fruits, you'll use either a "raw pack" or "hot pack" method, each of which involves packing the jars with fruit and boiling liquid (usually water). You'll find instructions for several types of produce later in this chapter and elsewhere in this book. Refer to page 119 for guidance on preparing and canning whole or cut-up fruit.

Step 7

After you fill a jar, release air bubbles from around the food by running a spatula or bubble releaser between the fruit and the jar. Make sure the rim and threads of the jar are clean. Use a damp cloth to remove any food that might have splashed when you filled the jar.

Step 8

Set a hot lid on the jar and screw a band down tightly. Don't pull a muscle, but apply more than just finger strength as you tighten it down.

After checking the headspace and cleaning the jar's rim, drop on a canning lid and then screw a band down relatively tight.

Step 9

Set each jar into the boiling water bath canner once you've applied the lid and band.

Don't tilt the jars when you lift them into your canning pot. In this photo, I'm lifting the jar by the flange below the ring. It's important not to pick up the jar by the band. In fact, don't disturb the band until 12 hours after the jars come out of the canner.

Step 10

When you've filled all the jars and placed them in the canner, evaluate the depth of the water and add more already boiling water, if necessary, to raise the surface at least 1 inch above the tops of the jars.

Step 11

Cover the canning pot and wait until the water returns to a rolling boil. Start timing and let the water boil for the number of minutes shown in the table on page 118. If the water stops boiling before the time is up, raise the temperature of the burner and bring the water back to a rolling boil. Start timing again for the total time noted in the table.

Step 12

When the time is up, remove the canner from the heat and remove the jars from the canner. Don't tip the jars as you move them to a cooling rack or a towel spread on a table or counter. Leave ½ inch or more of space between the jars so air can circulate freely.

Step 13

Let the jars cool until they reach room temperature, usually about 12 hours. In the first 10 minutes, each jar should seal. When that happens, the center of the metal lid pops downward and makes an audible pop or ping. That ping should become music to your ears: it's the first sign that your efforts were successful.

Step 14

Test the seals of the lids. On visual inspection, the lid should be concave, bowing downward in the middle. Unscrew each band and lift the jar by the edges of the lid. If the lid comes free, try one of the following:

• Apply a new lid and process the jar for the full time specified in the table on page 118.

• Store the unsealed jar (use the failed lid and band to keep it covered) in your refrigerator and use its contents within a week.

• Remove enough of the jar's contents to provide 1 ½ inches of headspace, apply the lid and band, and store the jar in your freezer. Use the contents within a year.

Step 15

Label properly sealed jars with the date and their contents. Store them in a cool, dark, dry place. Leave the bands off the jars; they may stick and become difficult to remove if you leave them on.

CAN TOO!
Extra

If you plan to reuse your canning jars season after season, don't apply stick-on labels to the jars. I use a permanent ink marker to write on the lid, which I'll discard eventually anyway. It's a royal pain to remove labels from the glass, and they can deteriorate in the dishwasher and plug up the mechanism.

Boil Jars to Save Effort

Some canning instructions require that you sterilize the jars before filling them, but for nearly everything you'll can, this step isn't necessary. To sterilize jars, you submerge them in water, bring them to a rolling boil, and let them cook for ten minutes or longer.

Though it isn't necessary, I always do this: I inspect and wash the jars and put them into the canning pot. I fill the pot with hot water, fully submerging the jars, cover the pot, and set it on the stove on high heat. While the water comes to a boil, I prepare the foods I plan to can.

After at least ten minutes at a boil, the jars are very hot, so they're not likely to crack when I add hot sauces, syrups, or water. Since I have to heat the canning pot anyway, this eliminates the need to run the dishwasher or otherwise heat the jars before filling them. It significantly simplifies managing the space in my small kitchen.

Canning High-Acid Foods

High-Acid Foods Processing Times

The times given in this table assume that you are within 1,000 feet of sea level. Review the section following this table for information about boiling water bath canning at higher altitudes.

FRUIT	PACKING METHOD	MINUTES OF BOILING PINTS	MINUTES OF BOILING QUARTS
Apples	Hot	20	20
	Raw pack produces inferior results		
Applesauce	Hot	20	20
Apricots	Raw	25	30
	Hot	20	25
Berries*	Raw	15	20
	Hot	15	15
Cherries	Raw	25	30
	Hot	15	20
Cranberries	Hot	15	15
Grapefruit	Raw	10	10
Grapes	Raw	15	20
	Hot	10	10
Nectarines	Raw	25	30
	Hot	20	25
Oranges	Raw	10	10
Peaches	Raw	25	30
	Hot	20	25
Pears	Raw	25	30
	Hot	20	25
Pineapple	Hot	15	20
Plums	Raw	20	25
	Hot	20	25
Rhubarb	Hot	15	15
Tomatoes	*Find processing times listed along with canning instructions for the type of tomato product you're preserving on pages 135–138.*		

* Berries refers to all types of berries: blackberries, raspberries, blueberries, currants, elderberries, mulberries, and so on.

HIGH-ALTITUDE PROCESSING TIMES

If you live more than 1,000 feet above sea level, add the cooking times specified in the following table to the times specified in the preceding table, "High-Acid Foods Processing Times."

Altitude	Minutes to Add
1,001 to 3,000 feet	5 minutes
3,001 to 6,000 feet	10 minutes
6,001 to 8,000 feet	15 minutes
8,001 feet and more	20 minutes

Preparing Fruits for Canning

Canning begins with harvesting or selecting produce that is ripe and undamaged. Don't can fruit that has passed its peak. In fact, you may prefer the results when you use fruit that is just becoming ripe.

Food Mills for Sauces and Baby Food

When you preserve a lot of produce, you spend hours cutting, coring, and peeling fruits and vegetables. The single greatest shortcut for some food processing chores is to use a food mill.

A food mill grates fruits and vegetables into a fine mash while simultaneously straining out tough parts such as peels, seeds, and stems. Most commercial applesauces have gone through food mills; hence their smooth, consistent textures. You can get a similar texture by pressing cooked apples through a strainer—or mashing them through a ricer—but a food mill takes less effort.

A manual food mill involves hand-turning a crank that pushes cooked produce against a grating surface. The ground produce oozes through holes in the grater and collects in a bowl or pot beneath it. You can buy food mill attachments for some stand mixers, or buy electric food mills. These effortlessly reduce cooked foods to the consistency of baby food.

I hand-crank a food mill to make applesauce and tomato sauce. I quarter and core apples, leaving the skins on. I simply quarter tomatoes. For both, after cooking the fruit, I put it through the mill to remove the skins and, in the case of tomatoes, to remove the seeds. This is an amazing time-saver.

Canning High-Acid Foods

Canning is cooking, and cooking softens fruit and vegetables. Amazingly, when you follow the USDA's processing guidelines exactly, fruits that go into jars dead-ripe are going to end up softer than commercially canned fruits you buy in a grocery store. (They will also taste noticeably more like fruit.)

So if you want your canned fruit to resemble store-bought canned fruit, harvest and can it when it's just becoming ripe. If you want a rare culinary treat, harvest and can fruits at their peak of ripeness.

You can put any cooked vegetable through a food mill to produce high-quality baby food. Do not can such vegetable mash! There are no proven home-canning times for homemade baby foods made from low-acid vegetables. Freezing, however, is a terrific preservation method, so please check out Chapter 4 for guidelines on freezing vegetables and fruit.

Baby food that you make by milling fruit is acceptable for boiling water bath canning. Peel, pit or core, and cut up the fruit, and put it through a mill. Fill 1-cup canning jars and process for twenty minutes according to the instructions in "Basic Steps for Boiling Water Bath Canning" that begin on page 112. Adjust processing time for altitude according to the "High-Altitude Processing Times" table on page 119.

Ascorbic Acid

Ascorbic acid is vitamin C. It is most useful in canning to prevent fruits from changing color while you're preparing them for the canning jars. Ascorbic acid is usually available in season at your local grocery store, or from canning suppliers. You can also buy ascorbic acid powder at a pharmacy.

To keep cut fruit (and some vegetables) from changing color, store it in a solution of ascorbic acid or lemon juice and then pour off the solution before processing the fruit. When I prepare fruit that may discolor, I fill a 4-gallon pot about halfway with cold water. I add 1 teaspoon ascorbic acid or ½ cup lemon juice for each gallon of water—so I use 2 teaspoons ascorbic acid or 1 cup lemon juice for the 4-gallon pot. Then, I let the fruit float until I'm ready to can it.

For all fruits, reject any pieces that are overripe or bruised. For larger fruits such as apples, peaches, pears, plums, and tomatoes, cut away bruises and insect damage, but still use the healthy flesh. Here are guidelines for preparing and canning specific fruits.

Apple Slices

Harvest/Buy: Use ½ bushel (about 20 pounds) to fill 7 quart jars, or 13 pounds to fill 9 pint jars.

Select: Choose a mixture of apple varieties that includes both sweet and tart apples. Firm, crispy varieties hold their shape and texture better than softer varieties do.

Prepare: Prepare an acid solution according to the instructions in the "Ascorbic Acid" box on page 120, and float the prepared apple slices in the solution as you work.

You can cook and pack the apples in water that is up to 30 percent sugar. The "Syrups for Canning Fruit" table on page 132 provides measurements for making the right amount of syrup. Prepare the water or syrup ahead and have it hot so it's ready for the apple slices.

Can: Drain the prepared apples and load them into a large pot along with the heated water or syrup. Bring the mixture to a boil, stirring intermittently to keep the apples from burning; boil for 5 minutes.

Fill canning jars with the cooked apples and add enough liquid to cover them. Leave ½ inch of headspace (the space between the top of the packed produce and the lip of the jar). Slide a chopstick down the inside of the jars to release the air bubbles, add the lids and bands, and process the jars according to the "High-Acid Foods Processing Times" table on page 118.

Prepping Fruit Is a Big Job

It takes me about three hours to quarter and core a half bushel of apples, leaving the skins on. I know this because I can fill a 4-gallon pot with sliced apples while watching a football game on TV. I guess it would take four or more hours to quarter, core, and peel a half bushel.

Canning High-Acid Foods

Because preparing the fruit is so time-consuming, start prepping before you start heating the canner. After I wash the jars, I submerge them in the canning pot and leave them as the water heats to boiling. Water in my canner, when filled nearly to the top, takes forty-five minutes or more to get to a rolling boil. If you preheat your jars in your dishwasher or sink, you only need to fill your canner halfway with water; it will thus take less time to get to a boil.

Applesauce

Harvest/Buy: Use ½ bushel (about 24 pounds) to fill 7 quart jars.

Select: Use a mixture of apple varieties that includes both sweet and tart apples. Soft varieties break down easily with less cooking. Some common commercial varieties I like are McIntosh, Rome, Cortland, and Jonagold. Of course, use whatever you can obtain.

Prepare: Prepare an acid solution as explained in the "Ascorbic Acid" box on page 120. Wash, quarter, and core the apples (but don't peel them), and float the quarters in the acidified water as you work. Stuff the container to the gills with apple quarters.

When the pot is full, pour off the water and then add back 1 cup of liquid: water, apple juice, or apple cider. Set the pot on the stove, put the heat on medium-low, cover the pot, and cook, stirring regularly to keep the apples from burning.

When all the apple quarters are soft, put them through a food mill. This creates a smooth sauce and removes the skins from the mix.

Place the sauce on low heat and add sugar to taste. I add about 2 cups, which translates to about ¼ cup per quart of finished sauce.

Can: While the applesauce is boiling or near boiling, fill hot canning jars with the mixture, leaving ½ inch of headspace. Add lids and bands, and process the jars according to the "High-Acid Foods Processing Times" table on page 118.

Applesauce Challenges

CANNING

I find it challenging to stir a half bushel of quartered apples in a pot. However, as they cook, apples near the bottom of the pot soften and occupy less space. The contents of the pot reduce by several inches, and you should be able to slip a spoon in and turn the mass of cooked, partly cooked, and raw apples. Do this every ten minutes or so to keep apples from burning.

If you'll be hanging out in the kitchen, you can turn the heat up to medium or medium-high and continue to stir regularly; the apples will cook in about an hour. If you want freedom, turn the heat very low and return every forty-five minutes or so to stir; it could take two, three, or even four hours to cook all the apples this way.

If It Sticks, Panic!

Actually, you don't need to panic, but it's important to act quickly if the apples stick to the bottom of the pot. As you stir, run the end of the spoon around the sides and against the bottom of the pot. If you feel resistance or if the spoon sticks in places, the cooking apples may start to burn. To prevent this, make one pass across the bottom of the pot, scraping with the spoon to the side of the pot. Continue this motion, dragging the spoon up against the side of the pot until it's clear of the apples. There are several possible scenarios:

- There is nothing unusual stuck to the tip of the spoon. Stir a bit more, scraping as much of the bottom of the pot as you can.

- There is a ball of cooked apple stuck to the tip of the spoon. Evaluate and proceed as follows:

  - The ball is apple colored or just a bit darker. Stir immediately, scraping the bottom of the pot thoroughly. Lower the heat and stir more often (always scraping the bottom) until all the apple quarters are soft.

  - The ball is very dark or even black. Remove the pot from the heat! Find another large pot and carefully (this stuff is hot) pour or scoop the cooking apples into this other pot. Do not scrape the bottom of the pot; there may be yummy-looking apple stuff stuck there, but under the good stuff is a layer of charcoal flavoring. Continue cooking the apples on lower heat in the new pot, stirring more often, and get all the way to the bottom when you do. Congratulations! You've just saved your applesauce from burning.

Mom's Spicy Applesauce

My mom ever so rarely tossed a handful of red-hot candies into a batch of applesauce she cooked up for dinner. The red-hots sweetened the sauce, turned it red, and added a spiciness that my brothers and I loved. Try it! After milling the apples, add one 4-ounce container of red-hots for each quart of sauce and stir until they dissolve. Add sugar, if you wish, to finish the sauce, and then can it.

I usually can this spiced applesauce in pints and hand some out as gifts. The rest my kids gobble enthusiastically.

Apricots, Peaches, and Nectarines

Harvest/Buy: Use about 18 pounds to fill 7 quart jars, or 11 pounds to fill 9 pint jars.

Select: Choose fruit that is perfectly ripe and that does not have obvious dents and bruises.

Prepare: These fruits darken when in contact with air, so prepare an acidified water bath according to the instructions in the "Ascorbic Acid" box on page 120. Remove the skins from apricots and peaches but not from nectarines. If you're processing apricots or peaches, bring a large pot of water to a boil—use a pot large enough so that you can submerge three or more fruits in it at once.

Except for nectarines, submerge the fruits in the boiling water for no more than one minute and quickly cool them in cold water. The skins should peel off easily; remove them.

For any of the three fruits, halve them or slice them into segments and remove the pits. Place the prepared fruit in the acidified water to prevent it from discoloring.

Cook and pack the slices or halves in water that is anywhere from 0 to 30 percent sugar. The "Syrups for Canning Fruit" table on page 132 provides measurements for making the right amount of syrup. Prepare the water or syrup in advance and keep it hot so it's ready to receive your halved or sliced fruit.

Can: Raw pack nectarines only; apricots and peaches don't raw pack well. To do this, drain the prepared fruit and pack pieces cut side down in canning jars. Add hot water or syrup to cover, leaving ½ inch of headspace.

Hot pack any of the fruits by first draining the pieces and loading them into a large pot along with the heated water or syrup. Bring the mixture to a boil and immediately pack the hot fruit into canning jars.

Place the halves cut side down in the jars; let the slices fall as they may. Add enough liquid to cover the fruit, leaving ½ inch of headspace (the space between the top of the packed produce and the lip of the jar). Slide a chopstick down the insides of the jars to release the air bubbles, add the lids and bands, and process the jars according to the "High-Acid Foods Processing Times" table on page 118.

Berries

This procedure applies to blackberries, blueberries, currants, dewberries, elderberries, gooseberries, huckleberries, loganberries, mulberries, and raspberries.

Harvest/Buy: Use one flat (8 quarts) to fill 7 quart jars, or 5 to 6 quarts to fill 9 pint jars.

Select: Choose fruit that is perfectly ripe.

Prepare: Wash the berries and remove any crushed or mushy fruit. Cap, core, or remove the stems, if necessary. Use scissors to cut off the heads and tails of gooseberries. Cook syrup, if you're using it, or heat water to use when packing jars. The "Syrups for Canning Fruit" table on page 132 provides measurements for making the right amount of syrup.

Can: You can raw pack any berries. First add ½ cup hot syrup or water to each canning jar, then fill with berries, shaking occasionally to help the berries settle. Add more syrup or water to cover the berries, leaving ½ inch of headspace. Slide a chopstick down the insides of the jars to release the air bubbles, add the lids and bands, and process the jars according to the "High-Acid Foods Processing Times" table on page 118.

If you prefer, hot pack blueberries, currants, elderberries, gooseberries, or huckleberries. To do this, bring a large pot of water to a boil. Add ½ cup hot syrup or water to each canning jar, then plunge the prepared berries into the boiling water for 30 seconds. Immediately fill the prepared jar with these lightly cooked berries and add hot syrup or water to cover, leaving ½ inch of headspace. Slide a chopstick down the insides of the jars to release the air bubbles, add the lids and bands, and process the jars according to the "High-Acid Foods Processing Times" table on page 118.

Canning High-Acid Foods

Cherries (Sour or Sweet)

Harvest/Buy: Get one flat (8 quarts) to fill 7 quart jars, or 5 to 6 quarts to fill 9 pint jars. If you're buying by weight, assume about 2½ pounds per quart. So you'll need about 22½ pounds to fill 7 quart jars, or about 14 pounds to fill 9 pint jars.

Select: Choose fruit that is perfectly ripe.

Prepare: Wash the cherries and remove any crushed or mushy fruit. You can leave the pits or remove them. I prefer to remove them before canning, and I rather enjoy doing so. If you leave the pits in, poke two small holes through the skin on opposite sides of each cherry so the cherries don't burst while cooking. You can use a pin or sewing needle to keep the holes small, but a sharp bamboo cooking skewer or a paring knife with a sharp tip is easier to handle; you'll have to decide whether the larger holes are acceptable.

Cook the syrup, if you're using it, or heat water to use when packing the jars. Consult the "Syrups for Canning Fruit" table on page 132 for measurements to make the right amount of syrup.

Can: To raw pack cherries, add ½ cup syrup or water to each canning jar, then fill with cherries, shaking occasionally to help the cherries settle. Add more syrup or water to cover the cherries, leaving ½ inch of headspace. Slide a chopstick down the insides of the jars to release the air bubbles, add the lids and bands, and process the jars according to the "High-Acid Foods Processing Times" table on page 118.

To hot pack cherries, measure the prepared fruit into a large pot and add ½ cup syrup or water for each quart of fruit. Heat this to boiling and fill canning jars with the hot fruit and liquid, leaving ½ inch of headspace. Apply the lids and bands and process according to the "High-Acid Foods Processing Times" table on page 118.

NOTE

My dad made wine from sour cherries and he left the pits in the lees (the mashed cherries) during the first fermentation. After he bottled the finished wine, he had it analyzed at the local university. They reported high cyanide content; cyanide had leached from the pits into the fermenting juice!

Pitting Cherries Isn't a Chore

As a kid, I spent many hours pitting cherries for my mom's pies and my dad's wine making projects. This was never a chore, and to this day I enjoy pitting cherries. Why? Because pitting cherries was (and remains) a fine excuse to tune into a sports event or a B movie I probably wouldn't otherwise watch.

I rinse 2 or 3 quarts of cherries at a time, drain them, and return the cherries to a large bowl. I take the cherries and a second, empty bowl to my favorite chair in the living room, cover my lap with a large towel, and set the two bowls in my lap. For this to work well, the bowls need to touch each other, and ideally one bowl should overhang the lip of the other bowl.

Here's the important part: I'm about to get my fingers dripping with sticky cherry juice. So I turn on the TV and switch to a program that's going to run for several hours. Depending on how the season is going, I may watch Wimbledon or the U.S. Open golf tournament.

To pit sour cherries, I pick up a cherry between my thumb and the adjacent two fingers. I point the top of the cherry toward the same fingers of my other hand. With both hands over the bowl holding the washed cherries, I squeeze the pit into my receiving fingers. Then I drop the pitted cherry into the second bowl and the pit into the first bowl, starting a pile of pits along one side of the bowl.

To pit sweet cherries, I hold a cherry in one hand and use a sharp paring knife to scribe a circle around the cherry's pit, cutting through the skin and flesh. Then I peel half the cherry away from the pit, and peel the pit away from the other half of the cherry. As with sour cherries, I make a pit pile in the first bowl, and drop the pitted cherry halves into the second bowl.

Canning High-Acid Foods

Cranberries

Harvest/Buy: Select 8 quarts to fill 7 quart jars, or 5 to 6 quarts to fill 9 pint jars.

Select: Choose cranberries that are ripe and firm.

Prepare: Wash the cranberries, removing any crushed or mushy fruit. Remove the stems. Prepare heavy syrup for a 9-pint load or a 7-quart load according to the "Syrups for Canning Fruit" table on page 132. Use a very large pot as you'll be adding all the prepared cranberries to it and boiling them in the syrup.

DANIEL'S Didja-Know?

Most seeded grapes are quite soft inside their skins and there's a huge textural difference between the skin and the fruit itself. The cooking that takes place during canning accentuates the textural difference. Ideally, use seedless grapes for canning and can them before they're ripe. If the skins and centers are similarly hard when they're cooked, the finished product will be more pleasant to eat (hence the suggestion to can underripe grapes).

Can: While the syrup is boiling, add the cranberries and stir. When the syrup returns to boiling, cook for 3 minutes. Spoon the cranberries out of the syrup and fill canning jars, leaving ½ inch of headspace. Add enough hot syrup to cover the cranberries, still leaving ½ inch of headspace. Slide a chopstick down the insides of the jars to release the air bubbles, add the lids and bands, and process the jars according to the "High-Acid Foods Processing Times" table on page 118.

Grapes

Harvest/Buy: Measure grapes by weight, obtaining 1 pound of fruit for each pint you intend to store, or 2 pounds for each quart.

Select: Choose grapes that are a bit underripe and firm. If you're canning grapes, harvest them about 2 weeks before you'd think they are ready to eat.

Prepare: Wash and stem the grapes, removing crushed and soft fruit. Make light syrup according to the "Syrups for Canning Fruit" table on page 132. If you wish to hot pack the grapes, bring a large pot of water to a boil; you'll blanch the grapes in this water before placing them in jars.

Can: To raw pack grapes, fill canning jars with whole fruit, leaving 1 inch of headspace. Then add hot syrup to cover the grapes. To hot pack grapes, submerge them in batches in boiling water. Let the water return to a boil, then continue cooking for 30 seconds. Immediately load the hot grapes into jars and follow the raw pack instructions. For either method, slide a chopstick down the insides of the jars to release the air bubbles, add the lids and bands, and process the jars according to the "High-Acid Foods Processing Times" table on page 118.

Grapefruits, Oranges, and Tangerines

Harvest/Buy: Use 1 pound to fill a pint jar, or 2 pounds to fill a quart jar. About two large oranges will fill a pint; a large grapefruit could fill a pint jar as well.

Select: Find fruit that is perfectly ripe and ready to eat.

Prepare: Wash and peel the fruit and separate the segments. (Handling produce that may have soil, insecticides, or microbes stuck to it can spread contamination to the clean fruit inside so it's safer to wash all produce even if you're going to peel it.) Remove the white rind from the segments and any connective strips. Try not to damage the sections. You'll pack these fruits with water or syrup, so before packing jars, prepare and heat the liquid according to the "Syrups for Canning Fruit" table on page 132.

Can: Raw pack these citrus fruits. Fill canning jars with segments, leaving 1 inch of headspace. Add hot syrup to cover. Slide a chopstick down the insides of the jars to release the air bubbles, add the lids and bands, and process the jars according to the "High-Acid Foods Processing Times" table on page 118.

Canning High-Acid Foods

Pears

Harvest/Buy: You'll need 2 to 3 pounds for each quart jar, or about 20 pounds to fill 7 quart jars.

Select: Choose fruit that's ready to eat. It's useful to understand that green pears will ripen very nicely on your kitchen counter. So it's okay to buy underripe pears several days ahead. If you want to can pears from your own trees, read "Ripening Pears" for suggestions on harvesting the best possible product.

Prepare: Mix acidic water according to the instructions in the "Ascorbic Acid" box on page 120. Wash, peel, halve, and core the pears. Float the prepared halves in the acidified water as you work.

Pack the pears in water or light to medium syrup. Consult the "Syrups for Canning Fruit" table on page 132 to prepare the right amount of syrup.

Can: Drain the prepared pears and add them into a large pot along with the heated water or syrup. Bring the mixture to a boil, stirring occasionally to keep the pears from burning; boil for 5 minutes.

Pack canning jars with the cooked pears and add enough liquid to cover. Leave ½ inch of headspace. Slide a chopstick down the insides of the jars to release the air bubbles, add the lids and bands, and process the jars according to the "High-Acid Foods Processing Times" table on page 118.

Ripening Pears

Pears that ripen on the tree often develop hard spots and crunchy crystals within their flesh. This puts pears in a rare class of fruits that come out better when they ripen on your kitchen counter than when they ripen on the plant.

Actually, you'll get the smoothest, most pleasing pears if you watch for the first full-sized pear to drop from your tree naturally. At this point, all the pears are likely still to be green. Harvest them! Store the picked green pears in a refrigerator set to about 40 degrees Fahrenheit.

Leave the pears to age for four to six weeks, checking for spoilage every few days and removing any pears that start to go bad. After four weeks, when you want fresh pears, remove several from the refrigerator and set them on your counter. They'll ripen up in two to five days, and they'll be smooth, juicy, and flavorful.

Plums

Harvest/Buy: You'll need just over 2 pounds for each quart jar, or about 16 pounds to fill 7 quart jars.

Select: Choose fruit that's ready to eat. Some varieties of plums are very sweet and others are very sour (taste them and you'll know which you have). You use the same steps to can both types, but consider using a medium syrup for sour plums and a light syrup or plain water for sweet plums.

Prepare: Stem and wash the fruit and pierce the skin on opposite sides with the tip of a knife. Alternatively, halve the plums and remove the pits. Can plums in water or light syrup. Consult the "Syrups for Canning Fruit" table on page 132 to prepare the right amount.

Can: Bring the water or syrup to a boil, add the plums, and wait for the fluid to boil again. Boil the fruit for 2 minutes, remove it from the heat, and let the plums steep, covered, for 20 minutes.

Pack canning jars with the cooked plums and add enough liquid to cover the fruit. Leave ½ inch of headspace. Slide a chopstick down the insides of the jars to release the air bubbles, add the lids and bands, and process the jars according to the "High-Acid Foods Processing Times" table on page 118.

Rhubarb

Harvest/Buy: You'll need 1½ pounds for each quart jar, or about 11 pounds to fill 7 quart jars.

Select: Choose firm stalks with a lot of color.

Prepare: Remove the leaves, trim the bottoms of the stalks, and wash the rhubarb. Cut the stalks into 1-inch sections and put them in a large saucepan with ½ cup sugar for every quart of prepared fruit. When juice accumulates in the bottom of the pot, cover it, turn the heat on low, and let the rhubarb and sugar mixture come to a boil.

Can: Fill canning jars with the boiling rhubarb sauce, leaving ½ inch of headspace. Slide a chopstick down the insides of the jars to release the air bubbles, add the lids and bands, and process the jars according to the "High-Acid Foods Processing Times" table on page 118.

Pineapple

Harvest/Buy: You'll need 3 pounds for each quart jar, or about 21 pounds to fill 7 quart jars.

Select: Get ripe, but not soft, fruit.

Prepare: Wash the pineapple, twist off the top, peel the fruit, and remove the seed cavities. Slice the softer fruit away from the hard core and cut into strips or

Canning High-Acid Foods

chop into small pieces. Consult the "Syrups for Canning Fruit" table below to prepare the right amount of syrup.

Bring the water or syrup to a boil in a large saucepan and add the pineapple. Return the liquid to a boil and let the pineapple simmer for 10 minutes.

Can: Fill canning jars with the hot pineapple, then add enough hot liquid to cover the fruit, leaving ½ inch of headspace. Slide a chopstick down the insides of the jars to release the air bubbles, add the lids and bands, and process the jars according to the "High-Acid Foods Processing Times" table on page 118.

Syrups For Canning Fruit

I like to preserve foods in ways that retain their natural characteristics as much as possible. In canning fruit, this means I try not to oversweeten or to dilute what I put in the jars. However, due to the availability of commercially canned fruit, we've become accustomed to fruits packed in heavy syrups, medium syrups, and light syrups, and more recently to a growing selection of fruits packed in their own juices.

This table recommends the amounts of water and sugar to combine to make various types of syrup for canning (and freezing). The 10 percent sugar syrup most accurately matches the sweetness of fruit, and I recommend using either it or water for canning fruit.

To make syrup, combine the water and sugar in a saucepan and bring it to a boil. When you raw pack, you'll pour the syrup into jars that you've already loaded with fruit. When you hot pack, you'll add the fruit to the boiling syrup and cook it for several minutes before spooning the fruit into jars and then topping it with the hot syrup.

PERCENT SUGAR	FOR 9 PINTS		FOR 7 QUARTS	
	Water	Sugar	Water	Sugar
10%	6½ cups	¾ cup	10½ cups	1¼ cups
20%	5¾ cups	1½ cups	9 cups	2¼ cups
30%	5¼ cups	2¼ cups	8¼ cups	3½ cups
40%	5 cups	3¼ cups	7¾ cups	5¼ cups
50%	4¼ cups	4¼ cups	6¾ cups	6¾ cups

CANNING U

Add Citric Acid for Safe Tomatoes

Tomatoes usually contain enough acid that they nearly qualify as high-acid produce. Some reach the mark handsomely while others fall short. Home canners must ensure the acidity of the tomatoes they can by adding a bit of acid to every jar.

Use citric acid powder, which is available where you buy canning supplies and at pharmacies. Add ¼ teaspoon citric acid powder to each pint jar of tomatoes and tomato products you can. Add ½ teaspoon citric acid to each quart jar.

Or use lemon juice to increase the acidity of your tomatoes. Add 1 tablespoon commercially bottled lemon juice to each pint jar, and 2 tablespoons to each quart jar.

Acidifying your canned tomato products is so important that I mention it also within the step-by-step instructions in this chapter.

Tomatoes

Tomatoes have their own section in this chapter for a few reasons.

- Tomatoes are the most popular produce for home gardeners.
- We traditionally use tomatoes in an enormous selection of dishes.
- We're accustomed to many styles of preserved tomatoes: whole peeled tomatoes, diced tomatoes, tomato sauce, puréed tomatoes, and tomato paste are all available in grocery stores. You can also find spaghetti sauce, pizza sauce, and taco sauce—all tomato-based products. Finally, tomatoes are a component of ketchup, barbeque sauces, salad dressings, salsas, and chili sauces.

That's a lot of ground to cover! But, I'm not covering all of it. This section explains how to can tomatoes and basic tomato sauce. With these in your larder, you can quickly make hundreds of tomato-based dishes throughout the winter and until fresh tomatoes are available next year.

Peel Tomatoes Quickly

When canning, work with tomatoes that are ripe enough that their skins peel off easily. But don't labor to remove the skins. Rather, use this time-honored technique and the skins nearly remove themselves.

1. Fill a medium-sized pot with enough water to submerge three or four tomatoes and bring the water to a boil.

2. Work with just a few tomatoes at a time. Float them in the boiling water for 30 to 60 seconds but no longer. The skins may split.

3. Transfer the tomatoes directly to a pot or bowl of cold water.

4. If the skin hasn't split on a tomato, gently insert the tip of a knife through the skin and lift to tear it. The skins should slide off easily, coming away in just a few pieces.

Canned Whole or Cut-Up Tomatoes

Harvest/Buy: You'll need 3 pounds for each quart jar, or about 21 pounds to fill 7 quart jars.

Select: Choose ripe tomatoes that are ready to eat.

Prepare: Wash and peel the tomatoes. Reject any bruised or overripe tomatoes.

You can pack tomatoes in water or tomato juice, or simply pack them in their own juice. The liquid you choose determines how long the canning jars must remain in the boiling water bath.

To *raw pack* tomatoes in water or tomato juice, bring the liquid to a boil; it should be boiling when you fill the canning jars. (You'll need to raw pack tomatoes if you want to can them in their own juice without added liquid, but you'll need to use a slightly different procedure from a typical raw pack. See the canning directions that follow.)

To *hot pack* tomatoes in water or tomato juice, put the prepared tomatoes in a large saucepan, add enough liquid to cover them, bring the liquid to a gentle boil, and maintain the boil for five minutes.

Can: Whatever method of packing you choose, add acid to each canning jar before you fill it with the tomatoes. For pint jars, put 1 tablespoon commercially bottled lemon juice or ¼ teaspoon citric acid powder in the bottom of the jar. For quart jars, use 2 tablespoons lemon juice or ½ teaspoon citric acid powder.

After adding the acid, fill the canning jars as follows:

Raw pack by placing prepared tomatoes in the acidified jars. If you're packing in water or tomato juice, pack the tomatoes tightly but without crushing them, and then pour the hot liquid into the jars. Cover the tomatoes, leaving ½ inch of headspace. If you're packing without added liquid, press the tomatoes into the jars firmly until liquid from the tomatoes fills the empty spaces; you may add a few more tomatoes per jar using this method. A jar is full when there's ½ inch of headspace above the tomatoes and liquid.

Hot pack the tomatoes you've cooked for five minutes at a slow boil by fishing them out of the hot liquid and filling the acidified canning jars. Ladle the hot liquid into the jars until there is ½ inch of headspace.

Whatever method of packing you've used, slide a chopstick down the insides of the jars to release the air bubbles. Add the lids and bands and process the jars as follows:

Canning High-Acid Foods

Packing Liquid	Pints	Quarts
Packed in water	40 minutes	45 minutes
Packed in tomato juice	85 minutes	85 minutes
No added liquid	85 minutes	85 minutes

Plain Tomato Sauce

A pleasant tomato sauce is thick, smooth, and free of seeds. You make sauce that meets these criteria by cooking tomatoes for several hours and straining out the big chunks. If you preserve sauce with no added seasonings, you can use it in any dish that calls for tomato sauce. This sauce then becomes the canvas on which you paint with Italian, Spanish, Mexican, and Indian seasonings.

I can about forty-six pints of tomato sauce each year, and it's not enough. Here's how to make your own:

Harvest/Buy: You'll need ½ bushel (about 26 pounds) to fill 9 pint jars.

Select: Choose fruit that is perfectly ripe and free of disease, cracks, broken skin, mold, and spoilage. Paste varieties of tomatoes will provide a higher yield of sauce. Among the best-known paste tomatoes are Roma and San Marzano. You'll probably find several varieties of each as well as dozens of other decent paste tomatoes.

What Is a Paste Tomato?

The ideal slicing tomato is about the width of a sandwich. It has a reasonable amount of meat and is typically rather juicy. Paste tomatoes usually aren't sandwich sized, but they are much meatier than slicing tomatoes. What's more, a good paste tomato contains very little juice (and few seeds). It takes far less time to cook down a pot of paste tomatoes than it does to cook down a pot of slicing tomatoes.

On the previous page is a slicing tomato great for sandwiches and salads. On this page is a paste tomato. Pound for pound, the paste tomato will make more tomato sauce.

Prepare: Wash the tomatoes and cut them into quarters or smaller pieces. Fill a large pot as you work—a 4-gallon pot should be large enough to hold all the tomatoes. Pile the tomatoes above the top of the pot if necessary to fit them all in.

Set the pot on medium-low heat and cook. Stir occasionally to keep the tomatoes from burning. After 1 to 2 hours, tomato juice will develop to cover the tomato pieces. Maintain a very slow boil, stirring regularly, until the contents of the pot decrease by at least a third but by no more than half. That 4-gallon pot will be half full.

Canning High-Acid Foods

Run the tomatoes through a food mill, being careful not to splash hot juice on yourself. Collect the milled juice and pulp in a clean pot, and discard the tomato skins and seeds. Set the pot of milled tomatoes back on the heat and continue to simmer until there is just over 1 gallon of sauce in it. Cooking the tomatoes from a full 4-gallon pot down to 9 pints may take 12 or more hours of cooking on very low heat.

Finally, you're ready to can the tomato sauce.

Can: While the tomato sauce is boiling or near boiling, put either ¼ teaspoon citric acid or 1 tablespoon commercially packaged lemon juice into each hot pint canning jar. Fill the jars with the sauce, leaving ½ inch of headspace. Add the lids and bands and process the jars for 35 minutes. Double the citric acid or lemon juice and increase the processing time to 40 minutes if you can the sauce in quart jars.

Using Tomato Sauce

Cooking tomato sauce for canning is subjective: do you boil off half of the original volume, three-quarters of it, or even more? I like to cook sauce down so it becomes quite thick—so I can use a spoon to make little mounds of sauce on the surface in the pot. This makes the sauce very strong; it has so much tomato flavor, I can cut it with water and it still tastes fine.

Even when you cook your tomato sauce as thick as I do mine, it will have a different consistency from commercial tomato sauce; it won't be as smooth and "creamy." If you prefer that texture, there are two things you can try:

• After you mill the tomato sauce and return it to the stove to cook (before canning), pare three or four medium-sized potatoes and cut them into 1-inch cubes. Drop them in the pot. Fish out and discard the potato cubes just before canning the sauce.

• When you open a jar of sauce to use in cooking, stir 2 teaspoons cornstarch into each pint, or 4 teaspoons into each quart. When the sauce warms, the cornstarch will cause it to thicken. Don't add cornstarch to the tomato sauce before you can it; that may change the sauce's characteristics enough to make boiling water bath canning unsafe.

Through the Gateway

As with most food preservation methods, the most complicated part of canning high-acid foods is preparing them for packaging. What makes this okay is that you trade off preparation time on canning day to reduce preparation time when you cook meals. When you taste the amazingly accurate fruit flavors of home-canned produce, I believe you'll agree that canning is worth the effort.

I hope that opening a jar of home-canned peaches, applesauce, or diced tomatoes will give you the same rush it always gives me. Especially if you manage a home kitchen garden, there's enormous satisfaction in making pizza or spaghetti sauce from your own store of home-grown, home-canned tomato sauce.

By putting up your first jars of fruit or tomato products, have you passed through the gateway? Are you ready to make jam and jelly? To ferment vegetables? To pickle cucumbers in vinegar? This chapter introduced the fundamentals of home canning. They'll take you far as you experiment with other methods of food preservation.

Chapter 6

Sugaring

Jams, Jellies, Syrups, and Candied Fruits

Sugar never spoils. If you keep sugar dry and out of the reach of insects, people will be able to consume it without ill effects several hundred years from now. People long ago learned that adding sugar to perishable foods slows the growth of microbes that might make the foods spoil.

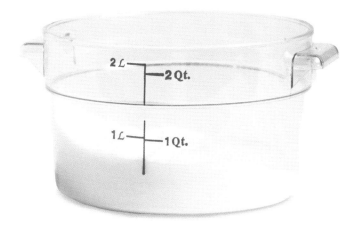

It's actually the combination of sugar and acid that has the best preservative effect: the acid already in fruit in combination with added sugar can extend the storability of fruit by many months.

I've dubbed the use of sugar as a preservative "sugaring." I learned the word as a kid when I participated with my family in maple sugaring—collecting sap from sugar maple trees and boiling it for hours to produce maple syrup. Historically, sugaring was a means of preservation in and of itself.

However, the USDA now tells us that popular methods of sugaring aren't reliable. They recommend that after you sugar a food, you use a secondary, more reliable method to ensure its long-term viability.

So while this chapter explains how to make jams, jellies, syrups, and candied fruits, each project ends with one of the other preservation methods: you can or freeze jams, jellies, and syrups, and you dehydrate or freeze candied fruits.

Sugaring

Foods to Preserve in Sugar

Sugaring is primarily about preserving fruit. When you prepare jelly and jam in the traditional way, you add an overwhelming amount of sugar to fresh fruit juice or fruit. Of course, making syrup is also about using a whole lot of sugar—usually with fruit, though you might also infuse syrups with herbs such as mint, lavender, or basil to flavor mixed drinks, to add to marinades and salad dressings, or to use as the base for savory-sweet sorbets.

You don't have to limit your sugaring to fruit-based products. You may candy vegetables as well as fruit, and some candied vegetables may play important roles in cooking. For example, some Asian dishes list candied ginger among their ingredients (I have friends who snack on candied ginger, citing medicinal benefits), and shavings from candied carrots or candied beets make unusual garnishes for salads and baked goods.

Jams and Jellies

Jam and jelly making are time-honored crafts. The aim is to combine the acid that occurs naturally in fruit with just enough sugar that microorganisms can't grow in the mixture. But if you combine just fruit and sugar, you get chunky syrup.

With just one more ingredient, pectin, chunky syrup makers can turn their fruity-sweet products into spreadable, sticky confections. Originally pectin came from floating green apples in the jelly pot, but we're fortunate today to be able to buy pectin in premeasured amounts that are just right for creating jams and jellies.

What Happened to Paraffin?

I've been involved in jelly making for more than forty years. While I didn't actually help my mother make jam when I was very young, I watched her, fascinated, as she filled the little jars and waited anxiously to see whether the jam would set. (The day you stop doubting that your jam will set is the day a batch of jam fails to set, leaving you with chunky syrup.)

After filling the jelly jars but while the jam was still hot, Mom would heat blocks of paraffin in a double boiler until they melted. Then she'd pour the wax gently onto the surface of the jam. As that cooled, it usually shrank away from the glass, so Mom would pour more melted paraffin on the jam.

When the jars finished cooling, the only barrier between the jam and the world was wax. These jars went into the larder, a closet in the basement where the temperature hovered around 65 degrees Fahrenheit most of the year.

Sometimes jam juice bubbled up around the edges of the wax. Sometimes mold formed on the wax (or on the bubbling jam juice). Did we throw out these jars of jam? No! When it was time for a new jar, Mom wiped off the mold and jam juice, removed the wax, and fed us the jam, and that was good enough for us, for pioneers, and for the United States Department of Agriculture.

Apparently, the USDA has found that eating jams and jellies preserved under paraffin can make you sick. So, please, if you're making a traditional cooked jam or jelly, put it in canning jars, cover it with canning lids and bands, and boil it for ten minutes according to the step-by-step instructions in this chapter.

NOTE

Mom stored opened jars of jam and jelly in the kitchen cabinet, not in the refrigerator (she did put lids on the jars). There is enough sugar in jam and jelly to keep harmful microbes from growing in it but not necessarily on it. Many is the time my mom scraped mold off jelly or jam and used what was left behind in our peanut butter and jelly sandwiches.

Sugaring

There are many brands of traditional fruit pectin, and most come in measured amounts with instructions for making one (nearly) perfect batch of jam or jelly. A traditional cooked jam or jelly will keep in a canning jar for more than a year without refrigeration. You can also use these brands of pectin to make freezer jam—a variation that tastes more like fresh fruit than traditional cooked jam, but that you must freeze if you want it to keep for a long time.

There are specialized pectin varieties for making low-sugar jams and jellies—and for making jams and jellies without cooking the fruit. Again, these may not have the staying power of traditional cooked jams and jellies. However, if you want jam but need to limit your sugar intake or you just don't want to fire up the stove, these more modern jelly-making methods might appeal to you. We'll look at traditional cooked jams and jellies and freezer jams in this chapter, but we're talking about sugaring, so we won't be making any low-sugar jam or jelly.

Traditional Cooked Jams and Jellies

To make a classic batch of jam or jelly, you need fresh fruit or fruit juice (see the "What's in Traditional Cooked Jam?" section on page 153), pectin, sugar, lemon juice (for some fruits), and jelly-making equipment (see page 145). Here's the trick, and it's hard to say this in a book about preserving food, but it's the best advice you'll ever get about making jam or jelly: buy some pectin and read the instructions in the package before you start.

Each brand of pectin provides estimates of how much fruit you'll need; terse instructions for preparing the fruit; specific measurements of sugar, lemon juice, and prepared fruit; cooking instructions; and cooking times. If you follow the instructions that come with the pectin, you'll create a great product nearly every time. (Honestly, I have never cooked a bad batch of jam or jelly. I follow instructions.)

So, please follow the recipes that come with the fruit pectin, but if you use the information in "What's in Traditional Cooked Jam?" you'll probably be happy.

Jelly-Making Equipment
(For Traditional Cooked Jelly)

For basic jelly and jam making, you need specific equipment.

Canning jars, lids, and rims. I fill 8-ounce jelly jars to give as gifts, and wide-mouth pint jars for jam and jelly we'll eat at home. We give a lot of jelly as gifts, so when I make a particular type of jam or jelly, I fill twelve gift jars.

CAUTION

Do you buy goods canned in glass jars from grocery stores? Mayonnaise? Pickles? Applesauce? Don't reuse those jars for jelly making or other home-canning projects; canning lids may not fit properly and the jars may crack or break when you heat them.

Do reuse jars specifically made for home canning. When I give canned goods as gifts, I mention to the recipients that I can refill the jars, so if they think of it, would they please save the jars for me (unless, of course, they have stuff they want to store in jelly jars).

Cooking pot that holds 2 gallons or more. You'll cook the jam or jelly in this pot. You'll never add even a gallon of ingredients, but when jam or jelly boils, it can quickly rise and spill over, and that's ugly. So use a much bigger pot than the ingredients would suggest, and still pay close attention when the heat is on.

Canning pot. If you don't have a canning pot, you can use a large cooking pot. The pot should be big enough to hold the jelly jars (standing up) that you plan to fill. It should also be deep enough so that when you fill it with water, you can submerge the jelly jars more than 1 inch beneath the surface.

Medium-sized saucepan. You'll heat the canning jar lids in water just below the boiling point. This pan needn't be huge, but it should be big enough to hold all the lids you'll use submerged in water.

Big spoon. You'll stir the jelly as it cooks, so the spoon's handle should be long enough that your hand doesn't have to cook as well.

Medium-sized bowl. This will hold sugar that you measure before starting to cook the jam. The bowl may need to hold as many as 7 cups of sugar.

Measuring cups. Use a liquid measuring cup for fruit juices and crushed or chopped fruit. Use a dry measuring cup for sugar.

Canning tools. A canning funnel makes it easy to put jam and jelly into canning jars. A jar lifter lets you easily handle hot jelly jars. I worked for years without these tools, but they are well worth the $7 or so you'll spend to buy a kit.

Cereal-sized heat-tolerant bowl. You may need to skim foam off your jam or jelly, so it's good to have a bowl handy.

Stainless steel measuring cup or ladle. I use a 1-cup measuring cup to scoop hot jam and jelly from the jelly pot into canning jars. A metal ladle would work as well.

Clean, damp dishtowel. If you splash jam or jelly on the rim of a jar, you need to wipe it clean before putting a lid on it.

Making Classic Cooked Jam or Jelly

Step **1**

Step-By-Step

Prepare the fruit or fruit juice according to the "What's in Traditional Cooked Jam?" section on page 153. If you're making jelly, it can take several hours to extract juice from fruit, so plan ahead.

Step 2

Wash and inspect the jelly jars, rejecting any that have cracks or chips or that have irregularities on the rim or threads.

About Yields

One in ten times, a jam or jelly recipe produces the amount of product predicted in the recipe. In one jam-making session, I made three batches of cherry jam, starting each with the same amount of fruit and sugar, and each yielded a different amount of jam. I've never ended up with less jam or jelly than a recipe estimates. So when preparing jars to hold the jam or jelly you're about to make, wash and heat enough jars to hold 1 pint more than the recipe predicts. When I make two batches in a row, I usually pour any extra from the first batch into that spare pint jar. Then when I make the second batch, I pour the pint jar into the cooking jam or jelly after I add the sugar, but before it starts boiling. This often produces enough in the second batch to fill a whole pint beyond the recipe's estimate with a bit left over for snacking later on.

Step 3

Fill the canning pot with hot water, add the canning jars, put a lid on the pot, and set it on high heat to boil.

Step 4

Wash the bands and lids and cover them with water in a medium-sized saucepan. Set the pan on the stove on low heat; by the time the water in the canning pot boils, the water with bands and lids should be very hot, but not boiling.

Step 5

Measure the sugar into a medium-sized bowl and set it within easy reach of the stove.

Measure the fruit or juice into the deep jelly-cooking pot. Then add the specified amount of lemon juice and the packet of fruit pectin (or you can use 1/3 cup—slightly heaping—bulk pectin such as Dutch Gel).

Boiling jam (and to a lesser extent, jelly) can produce foam that lingers after cooking. Skim this foam off and discard it (I eat it) before bottling the product. You can reduce the amount of skimming by adding 1/2 teaspoon butter to the pot as the jam cooks. I usually add butter after I've added the sugar but before the jam starts to boil for the second time.

Make sure the water in the canning pot is boiling before you start cooking the jam or jelly, then turn the heat under the jelly pot to its highest setting. Stir the mixture.

CAUTION

Never stop stirring the jam or jelly until you take it off the heat. Never stop stirring the jam or jelly until you take it off the heat. One more thought: never stop stirring the jam or jelly until you take it off the heat.

Stir. I slowly scrape the tip of the spoon in lazy circles and figure eights along the bottom of the pot. It may take 5 or 10 minutes of constant stirring, but keep going until the mixture boils. Then add the sugar all at once.

Stir. As you stir, feel for clumps of sugar and break them apart. If you don't break it apart, sugar can stay clumped and end up in the finished jam or jelly. Stir until the mixture begins to boil (it must boil even as you stir).

Seasoned Jams and Jellies

If you've never made jam or jelly, you might prefer to stick to the recipes and procedures described in this book and on boxes of pectin. Once familiar with the procedures, consider some simple tweaks to produce more flavors from the same recipes. One obvious tweak is to add cinnamon to just about any fruit jam or jelly. For a full batch, add as much as 1 tablespoon ground cinnamon before you start cooking the fruit or fruit juice. Other seasonings that work with just about any fruit are allspice, nutmeg, and cloves. As with cinnamon, use ground seasonings so you don't have to fish out little bits before you put the cooked jellies and jams in jars. For a particularly refreshing and unexpected flavor, crush a dozen or so star mints (peppermints) and add them to a pot of jam or jelly that you're about to start cooking. (Whole mints and very large chunks may not melt completely during cooking, so crushing the mints is an important step.) I especially like the combination of sour cherries and star mint candy cooked up as jam.

Step 10

Stir, and let the jam or jelly boil for 1 minute. Immediately remove the jelly pot from the heat.

If you stop stirring while jam is cooking, chunks of fruit can burn and get stuck to the bottom of the pot. This can impart a burned flavor to the jam. Don't scrape that stuff off and mix it in with the jam. Rather, keep the unstuck jam moving until it finishes cooking. Then mix a teaspoon or two of almond extract into the pot before you bottle the jam. The almond extract can mask or even eliminate the flavor of burning.

Skim any foam. Use the spoon to gather foam along one side of the pot, then scoop as much of it as you can off the liquid. I save the foam and snack on it later.

Fill the jars with the hot jam or jelly, leaving ¼ inch of headspace (the space between the top of the jam or jelly and the lip of the jar). With jam, try to get a reasonable amount of fruit in each jar. You may need to scoop liquid from under the fruit for the first few jars or some jars will end up being all fruit, while others are mostly jelly.

Cover the jars. After you fill a jar, wipe the rim and threads clean if you've splashed jam or jelly there. Then set a lid on the jar, shiny side up, and screw a band down on the lid. Screw the band on firmly; it needs to press the rubber sealant of the lid down onto the rim of the jar. Return the filled jar, upright, to the canning pot.

NOTE

When you remove a jar from the canning pot to fill it with hot jam or jelly, pour the water it contains down the sink. Otherwise, once you fill several jars with jam or jelly and return them to the pot, you may end up with too much water there, and it could overflow.

Step 14

When you set the last filled jar into the canning pot, make sure the tops of the jars are at least 1 inch below the surface of the water, and the water is still boiling. Cover the pot and let it boil for 10 minutes (adjust this time according to "Canning Jam at High Altitudes"). Remove the jars from the pot and set them on a cooling rack or a towel spread on the counter.

Canning Jam at High Altitudes

After bottling the jam or jelly, you should cook the jars in a canning pot of boiling water for 10 minutes. But this assumes you're within 1,000 feet of sea level. When you're at a higher altitude, adjust the time in the canning pot according to the following table.

ALTITUDE	TOTAL PROCESSING TIME
0 to 1,000 feet	10 minutes
1,001 to 3,000 feet	15 minutes
3,001 to 6,000 feet	20 minutes
6,001 to 8,000 feet	25 minutes
8,001 to 10,000 feet	30 minutes

Step 15

If you've made jam, monitor the jars. After they seal and are still hot, flip them tops-down and let them continue to cool. Check them every 30 minutes or so and when they're still very warm and the jam inside is liquid, flip them again. If you don't take these steps, the fruit pieces in the jam will likely float to the surface, leaving only jelly in the bottom of the jar.

Step 16

Test the lids to be sure they sealed. The center of the lid should bow down, and when you press on it, it should feel solid. An unsealed lid will pop downward when you press on it. If you find a jar that isn't sealed, use that jam or jelly first or change the lid and reprocess it in a boiling water bath for the full 10 minutes.

Step 17

Label the jars with the contents and date, and store them in a cool, dark place.

About Boiling Jam and Jelly

The sugar in jams and jellies makes them boil at a higher temperature than water does. This stuff is very hot and can burn skin off your hands, so show it respect. Once the liquid boils, it can rapidly foam up and overflow the pot. Stirring holds this down, but if the foam rises rapidly even while you're stirring, immediately lift the pot off the burner until the bubbling subsides.

What's in Traditional Cooked Jam?

The steps to cooking and canning traditional jams and jellies begin with "prepare the fruit or fruit juice." For each fruit or fruit combination listed, you'll see how much fruit to start with, how to prepare it for cooking, and how much of the prepared fruit (or juice) you'll need to make one batch of jam.

Apple

Jam: You'll need about 10 apples. Choose a firm variety such as Fuji, Granny Smith, or Cortland. Wash, peel, core, and dice the apples until you have 6 cups prepared fruit. Add ½ cup water before cooking. Use 5 cups sugar. Makes 7 cups.

Jelly: You'll need about 12 apples. Wash, core, dice, and put the apples in a saucepan along with 4 cups water. Cook them according to the instructions in the "Juice from Fruit for Jelly and Syrup" section on page 158. You'll need 5 cups extracted juice and 7 cups sugar. Makes 7 cups.

Apricot

Jam: Start with 3½ pounds of apricots. Wash, pit, and dice the apricots without removing the skins. Measure 5 cups prepared fruit into your jelly pot and add ¼ cup lemon juice. Use 7 cups of sugar. Makes 8 cups.

Jelly: Use 4 pounds of apricots. Wash and pit the apricots and cut into chunks. Add 1½ cups water before extracting juice as directed in the "Juice from Fruit for Jelly and Syrup" section on page 158. Measure 4 cups extracted juice into your jelly pot along with ¼ cup lemon juice. Use 5½ cups sugar. Makes 6 cups.

Blackberry

Jam: Start with 2 quarts of blackberries. Wash the berries and crush them with a potato masher. Measure 5 cups prepared fruit into your jelly pot and add ¼ cup lemon juice. Use 7 cups sugar. Makes 8 cups.

Jelly: Start with 4 quarts of blackberries. Wash and juice the berries according to the instructions in the "Juice from Fruit for Jelly and Syrup" section on page 158. You'll need 4 cups extracted juice as well as ¼ cup lemon juice. Use 5½ cups sugar. Makes 6 cups.

Blueberry

Jam: You'll need 1½ quarts of blueberries. Wash the berries, pick out the stems, and crush the berries. Measure 4 cups prepared fruit into your jelly pot along with 2 tablespoons lemon juice. Use 4 cups sugar. Makes 6 cups.

Jelly: You'll need 2 quarts of blueberries. Wash the berries, add 1 cup water, and juice them according to the instructions in the "Juice from Fruit for Jelly and Syrup" section on page 158. Measure 3 cups extracted juice into your jelly pot along with ¼ cup lemon juice. Use 4 cups sugar. Makes 5 cups.

Sugaring

Cherry (Sour)

Jam: Start with 3 quarts of cherries. Wash, stem, and pit the cherries, and chop them into small pieces, preserving the juice. Measure 4 cups prepared fruit and juice into your jelly pot. Use 5 cups sugar. Makes 6 cups.

Jelly: Start with 3½ quarts of cherries. Wash, stem, and pit the cherries, and chop them into small pieces. Extract the juice according to the instructions in the "Juice from Fruit for Jelly and Syrup" section on page 158. Measure 4 cups extracted juice into your jelly pot. Use 5½ cups sugar. Makes 6 cups.

From the Tip Jar

Technically, you don't need to stem and pit cherries if you're juicing them for jelly. However, once you've extracted the juice, the remaining chopped cherries are still edible and quite begging to end up in your diet. So when you make cherry jelly, stem and pit the cherries, extract the juice, and then use the nearly juiceless chopped cherry bits to make something tasty to eat. I've made cherry pies from these leftover bits. See "Chopped Cherry Pie" on page 161 for one filling recipe. Instructions for making pies begin on page 93 in Chapter 4.

Cherry (Sweet)

Jam: Start with 3 quarts of cherries. Wash, stem, and pit the cherries, and chop them into small pieces, preserving the juice. Measure 4 cups prepared fruit and juice into your jelly pot and add ¼ cup lemon juice. Use 5 cups sugar. Makes 6 cups.

Jelly: Start with 3½ quarts of cherries. Wash, stem, and pit the cherries, and chop them into small pieces. Extract the juice according to the instructions in the "Juice from Fruit for Jelly and Syrup" section on page 158. Measure 4 cups extracted juice into your jelly pot along with ¼ cup lemon juice. Use 5½ cups sugar. Makes 6 cups.

Elderberry

Jelly: You'll need about 3 pounds of elderberries. Wash the berries and remove the stems. Extract the juice according to the instructions in the "Juice from Fruit for Jelly and Syrup" section on page 158. Measure 3 cups extracted juice into your jelly pot along with ¼ cup lemon juice. Use 4 cups sugar. Makes 4 cups.

Grape

Jam: Start with 4 pounds of grapes. Wash the grapes and remove the stems.

For grapes with seeds, squeeze the grapes out of their skins and chop the skins into tiny pieces. Add 1 cup water to the skinless grapes, bring them to a boil, and simmer, covered, for 5 minutes. Press the cooked grapes through a strainer or food mill to remove the seeds, and then add the chopped skins back to the cooked, seedless grape pulp.

For seedless grapes, run batches through a food processor or a meat grinder to produce a pulpy mash. Add 1 cup water, heat to a boil, and simmer the mash, covered, for 5 minutes. Though the grapes are seedless, your jam will have a more pleasing texture if you press the cooked mash through a strainer or food mill.

Measure 6 cups prepared fruit into your jelly pot. Use 7 cups sugar. Makes 9 cups.

Jelly: Start with 4 pounds of grapes. Wash the grapes and remove the stems. Add 1½ cups water and extract the juice as directed in the "Juice from Fruit for Jelly and Syrup" section on page 158. Measure 5 cups extracted juice into your jelly pot. Use 6 cups sugar. Makes 8 cups.

as directed in the "Juice from Fruit for Jelly and Syrup" section on page 158.

Mulberry

Jelly: Follow the proportions and procedures for making blackberry jelly. I don't recommend mulberries for making jam.

Peach

Jam: Use 3 pounds of peaches. Wash and peel the peaches, then cut chunks from around the pit. I cut four or five lines around the fruit all the way into the pit. Then I cut four or five lines across the original cuts, also into the pit; this essentially dices the fruit. Remove the chunks from the pit and measure 4 cups into your jelly pot. Mash the peach chunks and add ¼ cup lemon juice. Use 5½ cups sugar. Makes 6 cups.

Jelly: Start with 4 pounds of peaches. Wash the peaches (there's no need to peel them) and cut chunks from around the pits (as directed for peach jam). Add 1½ cups water, and extract the juice as directed in the "Juice from Fruit for Jelly and Syrup" section on page 158. Measure 4 cups extracted juice into your jelly pot and add ¼ cup lemon juice. Use 5½ cups sugar. Makes 6 cups.

NOTE

I love the flavors of raspberries, blackberries, elderberries, and mulberries, but I really don't care for the crunch (or for seeds stuck between my teeth). Making jelly is the perfect way to eliminate the seeds while preserving the delicious flavor of the fruit.

Sugaring

Pear

Jam: You'll need 4 pounds of pears. Wash, peel, core, and dice the pears. Measure 5 cups prepared fruit into your jelly pot and add ¼ cup lemon juice. Use 7 cups sugar. Makes 8 cups.

Jelly: Start with 3½ pounds of pears. Wash and core the pears, chop them into small pieces (there's no need to remove the skin), and add 3½ cups water. Extract the juice according to the "Juice from Fruit for Jelly and Syrup" section on page 158. Measure 4 cups extracted juice into your jelly pot and add ¼ cup lemon juice. Use 5½ cups sugar. Makes 6 cups.

Plum

Jam: You'll need 4 pounds of plums. Wash, pit, and dice the plums. Add ½ cup water, bring the fruit to a boil, cover, and simmer for 5 minutes. Measure 6 cups prepared fruit into your jelly pot. Use 8 cups sugar. Makes 9 cups.

Jelly: Start with 5 pounds of plums. Wash, pit, and chop the plums, and add 1½ cups water. Extract the juice according to the instructions in the "Juice from Fruit for Jelly and Syrup" section on page 158. Measure 5½ cups extracted juice into your jelly pot. Use 7½ cups sugar. Makes 8 cups.

Raspberry

Jam: Start with 2½ quarts of raspberries. Wash and crush the berries. Measure 5 cups prepared fruit into your jelly pot and add 2 tablespoons lemon juice. Use 7 cups sugar. Makes 8 cups.

Jelly: Start with 4 quarts of raspberries. Wash and juice the berries according to the instructions in the "Juice from Fruit for Jelly and Syrup" section on page 158. You'll need 4 cups extracted juice along with ¼ cup lemon juice. Use 5½ cups sugar. Makes 6 cups.

Rhubarb

Jam: You'll need about 2 pounds of rhubarb. Wash the rhubarb and cut the stalks into ¼- to ½-inch lengths. Add ½ cup water and cook, covered, until the rhubarb begins to break down. Measure 5 cups prepared rhubarb into your jelly pot. Use 7 cups sugar. Makes 8 cups.

Jelly: Start with 3 pounds of rhubarb. Wash the rhubarb and cut the stalks into ¼- to ½-inch lengths. Add 1½ cups water and extract the juice as directed in the "Juice from Fruit for Jelly and Syrup" section on page 158. Measure 4 cups extracted juice into your jelly pot. Use 5½ cups sugar. Makes 6 cups.

Strawberry

Jam: You'll need about 2 quarts of strawberries. Wash the berries, remove the caps, and mash the berries (I use a potato masher). Measure 5 cups prepared fruit into your jelly pot and add ¼ cup lemon juice. Use 7 cups sugar. Makes 8 cups.

Jelly: Start with 3 quarts of strawberries. Wash the berries and extract the juice according to the instructions in the "Juice from Fruit for Jelly and Syrup" section on page 158. (There's no need to cap the berries before juicing them.) Measure 4 cups extracted juice into your jelly pot and add ¼ cup lemon juice. Use 5½ cups sugar. Makes 6 cups.

Strawberry-Rhubarb

Jam: Start with 2 quarts of strawberries and 1 pound of rhubarb. Wash the produce, hull the strawberries, and chop the rhubarb stalks into very small pieces. Measure 2 cups mashed strawberries, 2 cups chopped rhubarb, and ¼ cup lemon juice into your jelly pot. Use 5½ cups sugar. Makes 6 cups.

Juice from Fruit for Jelly and Syrup

I've always seen beauty in this simple technique of extracting juice for making jelly. Whatever fruit you're using, the steps are quite similar. First, make a jelly bag. Wait! Jelly bag? You can find jelly bags at cooking suppliers or you can fashion your own out of cheesecloth. I encourage you to do neither. My approach is a tad more amusing (but just a tad). At the beginning of jelly season, look through your shirt drawer for a T-shirt you can't remember having worn in the past year. The T-shirt must pass several simple tests:

- Are both the front and rear panels of the shirt free of holes? It's okay if there are holes in the sleeves, the armpits, and around the collar.

- Is the shirt clean? After you've washed it, will it gross you out to eat food that once came in contact with the shirt?

- Does the shirt have so little sentimental value that you'd be willing to use it to degrease your kitchen?

Step  **1**

Rinse the fruit and remove overripe and spoiled pieces.

Step 2

Remove pits or cores if there are any, and cut larger fruits (apples, apricots, pears, peaches, pineapples, plums) into pieces. I usually cut such fruits into 1-inch chunks.

Step 3

Abuse the fruit. My implement of choice for this is a potato masher. It's ideal for smooshing fruit chunks or berries against the bottom of a pot. Crush the fruit until you can't spot any of the original fruit chunks or berries.

For firm fruits such as apples and pears, cook the fruit for 10 minutes until it softens, then mash it and cook it for a few more minutes. The "What's in Traditional Cooked Jam?" section on page 153 identifies fruits to which you should add water before cooking.

Step 4

Cook the fruit. Unless otherwise stated for a specific fruit, bring the crushed fruit to a gentle boil in a covered pot and let it simmer for 10 minutes.

Step 5

Pile the cooked fruit mash into a jelly bag and collect the juice.

To extract juice from the cooked fruit mash, follow these steps:

Step 1

Soak the clean, soon-to-become-unwearable T-shirt with water and wring it out so it's thoroughly damp.

Step 2

Lay the damp shirt over a bowl or pot that is large enough to contain all the cooked fruit mash. The shirt's back or front panel should face up and should cover the entire rim of the bowl or pot. Push the shirt down in the middle so it more or less lines the inside of the container.

Pour the still hot mash onto the shirt. Try to pour slowly and gracefully; many fruit mashes stain and it's easy to splash mash when you pour it this way.

Gather the shirt from around the rim of the bowl or pot and pull it together (gently) to form a bag around the fruit mash. Wrap a loop of twine around the gathered shirt and cinch it so that it holds the bag closed. Do not squeeze the bag you've created.

Lift your homemade jelly bag by the string, keeping the bag centered over the bowl or pot in which you formed it. Hang the string on the doorknob of a cabinet, keeping the bowl underneath. (What a relief that you didn't opt for those knobless cabinet doors, hey?)

IMPORTANT

Don't squeeze the jelly bag. That can force particles through the cloth and result in cloudy juice; cloudy jelly won't win ribbons at the county fair.

After 2 or 3 hours (I often leave mine to drip overnight), measure the juice. Did you get as much as the instructions suggested you would? Too little? Been there. But understand this: the instructions promised a specific amount of fruit would produce a specific amount of juice. If you got less juice than promised, the fruit owes you more. So load the juice that has collected into a container for the refrigerator. Then take down the jelly bag, set it in the bowl or pan where it started, and gently unwrap it. Add hot water to the mash—about ¼ cup more water than juice you need—and gently mix it in with the mash. Let it sit for several minutes.

Gather the shirt into a bag, tie it with string, and hang it once again over the collection bowl or pot. After 2 or 3 hours, add the newly acquired juice to the earlier batch in your refrigerator, discard the mash, and clean up the shirt for your next batch of jelly juice.

Chopped Cherry Pie

There's no greater culinary travesty than throwing away perfectly good food. Still, many jelly makers do exactly that. After extracting the juice from fruit, they toss the leftover mash into the compost bin or, worse, into the trash.

For some mashes, I applaud this action; I've no interest in the seedy mass left from juicing raspberries or in the mushy pulp left from juicing peaches, pears, and apples. However, after juicing cherries, I love to use the leftover chopped cherry mash to make pies.

In Chapter 4, I explain how to make fresh fruit pies that you can freeze. To make a pie with chopped cherry mash, treat the cherry mash as you would apples. The cherries are very dry, having given up their juice for jelly, so you need only a little thickener—use 3 tablespoons flour. Sweeten with 1¼ to 1½ cups sugar.

Or use the cherry mash in a custard pie filling. In a large bowl combine 1½ cups sugar with 3 tablespoons flour. Then whisk together 1 cup milk and 2 eggs. Add the milk and egg mixture to the sugar and flour mixture, and stir until all the ingredients are blended. Add 3 cups chopped cherry mash to the custard mixture and toss to mix. Pour the mixture into a piecrust, add a lattice top, and bake at 400 degrees Fahrenheit for 40 minutes or until the crust is golden brown.

Sugaring

When Jam or Jelly Doesn't Set

Most of the jam and jelly I make sets as quickly as it cools. However, some mixtures can take as long as four weeks to set up, though I start getting uneasy if they haven't set after two weeks.

If your jam or jelly doesn't set, it will be great on ice cream, on pound cake, and on cheesecake. However, if only jam or jelly will do, you can reprocess your preserves to encourage them to set. Here's how:

1. Count the number of cups of jam or jelly to reprocess, open the sealed jars, and empty them into your jelly pot.

2. You're going to can the reprocessed jam or jelly as you did when you first made it, so rinse the jars in hot water till they're clean and set them in a deep pot of water on high heat. Set an equal number of new (unused) canning lids in a small saucepan of water on low heat. Wait for the water in the canning pot to boil.

3. For each cup of product to reprocess, measure and set aside 2 tablespoons sugar. Then measure 1 teaspoon fruit pectin and 1 tablespoon water into a small saucepan and bring it to a boil, stirring continually to keep it from burning.

4. Stir the hot liquid pectin into the product in your jelly pot, add the sugar, and bring it all to a boil. Stir constantly while the jam or jelly is cooking, and cook it at a full boil for 30 seconds.

5. Remove the reprocessed jam or jelly from the heat and skim the foam if there is any. Fill the jelly jars, apply the lids and bands, and boil them submerged in water for 10 minutes.

6. Cool the jars on a towel or a cooling rack.

Freezer Jam

Freezer jam doesn't require the high-temperature cooking of traditional jam; freezer jam also retains the flavor of fruit better than traditional cooked jams do. In addition, freezer jams are easier to make, so the introduction of this jam-making method brought more people into the food-preserving community.

The downside of freezer jams is that they require refrigeration. For immediate use, you store them in the refrigerator. For long-term storage, they must go in the freezer. Chapter 4 explains the disadvantages and risks of freezing as a means of preservation.

To make freezer jam, you need fresh fruit (prepared properly as directed in the "Fruit for Freezer Jams" section on page 164), pectin, sugar, lemon juice (for some fruits), and equipment for making freezer jam (see the box on page 163). As with traditional cooked jams, please buy some pectin and read the directions in the box. The directions vary from one manufacturer's pectin to another's; maybe there are differences in the pectin that require differences in the recipes.

EQUIPMENT FOR MAKING FREEZER JAM

Freezer jams are easier to make than traditional cooked jams. Consequently you won't need as much equipment to make them.

Mixing bowl. You'll be stirring together a whole lot of fruit and sugar, so use a bowl that holds at least 6 quarts.

Measuring cups. Use a liquid measuring cup for crushed or chopped fruit. Use a dry measuring cup for sugar.

Mixing spoon. You might use a spoon to mix sugar with the fruit, and again to mix pectin with the fruit and sugar.

Small pot. You do need to cook a bit to make freezer jam; you heat a small amount of water and dissolve the pectin in it, kind of like when you make gelatin.

Freezer containers. Canning companies make containers specifically for freezing. You can use other food-storage containers, but some get brittle when cold and may break if you try to open them right after they come out of the freezer. I wouldn't give freezer jam as a gift, so I put mine into pint-sized freezer containers; we go through a pint of jam easily in three weeks.

Stainless steel measuring cup or ladle. I usually just pour the finished jam from the mixing bowl directly into freezer containers, but sometimes I use a 1-cup measuring cup to scoop jam into containers. A metal ladle would work as well.

Six Steps to Making Freezer Jam

1. Wash the freezer containers and have them ready to receive the mixed jam. They need not be hot when you fill them later.

2. Place the prepared fruit (see the "Fruit for Freezer Jams" section on page 164 for measurements and preparation) into the mixing bowl and add lemon juice (if needed) and sugar.

3. Mix the sugar and fruit thoroughly and let it stand for 10 minutes or more while you prepare the pectin.

4. Mix ¾ cup water and one package fruit pectin (alternatively, use ⅓ cup bulk pectin such as Dutch Gel) in the pot. Stir and heat the mixture to a boil that won't stop as you're stirring it. Boil the mixture hard while stirring for 1 minute, then immediately remove it from the heat.

5. Add the hot pectin to the bowl of sugared fruit and stir for 3 minutes.

6. Fill the freezer containers, leaving ½ inch of headspace (clearance between the top of the jam and the lid of the container). Label the containers and put them in the refrigerator until the jam sets, then move the containers to your freezer. The jam will keep for about 3 weeks in your refrigerator, and for a year or longer in your freezer.

Fruit for Freezer Jams

Freezer jam recipes abound that specify various proportions of fruit to sugar, but you can usually achieve satisfactory results by following one basic formula: start with 2 cups prepared fruit, 1 package (or ⅓ cup) powdered fruit pectin, 4 cups sugar, and 2 tablespoons lemon juice.

To make 2 cups of prepared fruit, you'll need 4 to 6 cups of fresh fruit (strawberries tend to smash down more than blueberries do). Follow the instructions in the "What's in Traditional Cooked Jam?" section on page 153 to prepare the fruit. Use half of the suggested water (if any), and add only 2 tablespoons lemon juice, no matter what those instructions tell you.

You're making freezer jam, so follow instructions to prepare fruit for jam. If you want to try making freezer jelly, prepare juice as directed in "What's in Traditional Cooked Jam?" on page 153. Make your jelly using 2 cups extracted juice, 1 package pectin, 4 cups sugar, and 2 tablespoons lemon juice. Since juice extraction typically involves cooking the fruit, the flavor of freezer jelly isn't much different from that of traditional cooked jelly.

Too Much Jelly? Cook!

My family gives away a lot of homemade jam and jelly: at least sixty 1-cup jars every year. Still, at the beginning of the next fresh fruit season, I have a lot left in my larder. I find many ways to use jam and jelly in cooking. Here are two of my favorites.

Peanut Butter and Jelly Cookies

Use a dark jelly or jam for twenty cookies, and a light color for another twenty, then put both types on a platter for guests.

Makes 40 large cookies (but if you make ¾-inch dough balls, you can get 60)

1 stick butter at room temperature

½ cup smooth peanut butter

½ cup raw sugar (white sugar is okay too)

½ cup brown sugar

2 eggs

1 teaspoon vanilla extract

¼ teaspoon baking soda

Pinch of salt

2 cups all-purpose flour

Your favorite jam or jelly

Sugaring

Beat the butter, peanut butter, and sugars in a large bowl until creamy. Add the eggs and vanilla and mix until smooth. In a separate bowl mix the baking soda and salt through the flour. Gradually add the dry mixture to the wet mixture, blending to make a very soft dough.

To make a cookie, roll about 1 tablespoon dough between your hands to create a 1-inch ball. Roll the ball in sugar and place it on a greased cookie sheet. Press your thumb into the middle, making a bowl. Try to leave the center of the cookie about ¼ inch thick.

Put a dollop of jam or jelly in the thumbprint—about ½ teaspoon. Space the cookies 1 inch apart. Bake at 375 degrees F for 13 minutes. Let the cookie sheet cool for a few minutes before transferring the finished cookies to cooling racks.

After cooling, the cookies will draw moisture out of the jelly; they can become very moist and soft in about a day. To prevent this, I freeze my peanut butter and jelly cookies, thawing just the ones I'm about to serve.

I make peppermint-cherry jelly specifically to use on thumbprint cookies. Crush enough star mints to fill a measuring cup, and replace 1 cup of the sugar in the jelly recipe with 1 cup crushed mints. If any mint pieces don't fully dissolve while cooking, try to fish them out as you fill the jelly jars.

Jelly Crepes

A crepe is a cross between a pancake and a noodle; at least, that's how I think of it. Crepes are amazingly easy to make, and they instantly impart a gourmet touch to whatever you wrap in them. Professionally trained chefs may cringe at my methods—I've never read a crepe recipe—but my family seems to like the results and I can't imagine an easier way to make these delicacies.

Makes 8 to 10 seven-inch crepes

1½ teaspoons baking powder

Pinch of salt

1 cup all-purpose flour

2 tablespoons butter, melted

1 cup milk

4 eggs

Vegetable oil

Neufchâtel cheese at room temperature

Jam or jelly of your choice

In a medium-sized bowl mix the baking powder and salt through the flour. Then add the melted butter and milk and stir (I use a whisk) until well blended. Add the eggs and mix until you have a smooth, thin batter.

To cook a crepe, use a 7-inch nonstick omelet pan or a properly seasoned cast-iron pan. Wipe the inside of the pan with a very thin coating of oil and set it on medium-high heat. When the pan is hot, spoon nearly 3 tablespoons (slightly less than ¼ cup) batter into it. Immediately pick up the pan and tip it from side to side so the batter flows across the bottom; try to distribute the batter evenly as it cooks.

Sugaring

This should take about 1 minute. Peel up the crepe along one edge, work a spatula under it, and flip it. The cooked side should be yellow with patches of golden brown. Let it cook for about 1 minute, at which point it should easily shake loose from the pan.

Transfer the crepe to a plate, spread one side of it with cheese, and spread about 2 tablespoons jam or jelly over half the crepe. Starting at the jellied edge, gently roll up the crepe. The jelly will distribute itself across the second half of the crepe as you roll it up. Repeat to make the rest of the crepes.

Place two rolled crepes on a plate, dust with powdered sugar, and serve.

Syrups

A good fruit syrup has a surprising number of uses. For example, I use fruit syrups on pancakes, waffles, and French toast and as toppings for ice cream and shaved ice. I also use fruit syrup to flavor custard that I freeze into homemade ice cream—one of my sons is particularly enthusiastic about homemade black raspberry ice cream. If you don't make ice cream, you can still scoop some into a blender with milk and homemade fruit syrup to produce refreshing milk shakes that rival those of the local ice cream shop.

Fruit syrups are crucial ingredients in many mixed drinks, and if you enjoy making your own cocktails, having homemade fruit syrups on hand will likely lead to many inventions that please your palate. See the "Mixology" box on page 170 for ideas to get your experiments started.

Fruit syrups make terrific additions to marinades, barbecue sauces, salad dressings, and salsas. If you don't usually make your own fruit syrup, start experimenting by replacing honey, corn syrup, molasses, or other liquid sweeteners in familiar recipes with your own homemade fruit syrups. The "Black Raspberry Teriyaki" on page 171 presents a marinade that is a proven winner with my family for both chicken and beef.

Making and Canning Fruit Syrups

When you mix 1 cup water with 1 cup sugar, you create a simple syrup. This is approximately the proportion of sugar to water that you find in pancake syrup, and this mixture is reasonably immune to colonization by microorganisms. If you were to leave a covered jar of simple syrup in your kitchen cabinet, it would likely remain unspoiled for years.

You improve the odds when you acidify your simple syrup and use a boiling water bath canner to hermetically seal it in jars. This is not a rigorous exercise; there is no minimum or maximum amount of fruit to buy or syrup to make. I usually buy fruit in bulk (a flat of sour cherries, for example) and end up with an odd quart or so that I'll use to make syrup.

1. Whatever amount of fruit you have on hand, follow the procedures in the "Juice from Fruit for Jelly and Syrup" section on page 158 to make fruit juice. Adjust the amount of water you add according to the amount of fruit you start with. So, for example, if you're making blueberry syrup from only 1 quart of blueberries, add just $\frac{1}{2}$ cup water rather than the full cup called for when you juice 2 quarts of berries.

2. Measure the extracted juice into a saucepan. You'll be adding an equal amount of sugar to this juice, but that won't double the amount of product. Still, in the next few steps, prepare enough canning jars and lids to handle twice the syrup as you have juice. That is, if you have $1\frac{1}{2}$ cups juice, prepare three 1-cup canning jars, or one pint jar and one cup jar.

3. Inspect the canning jars, rejecting any that have cracks or chips. Wash the jars.

4. Fill the canning pot with hot water, add the canning jars, put a lid on the pot, and set it on high heat to boil. If you're making only one or two jars of syrup, use the smallest pot you have that will hold the jars and still let you cover them 1 inch or deeper in water.

5. Wash the bands and lids and cover them with water in a medium-sized saucepan. Set that on the stove on low heat; by the time the water in the canning pot boils, the water with bands and lids should be very hot, but not boiling.

6. When the water in the canning pot is boiling, set the juice on a burner and bring it to a full boil.

7. Measure as much sugar as you measured juice earlier, and add the sugar to the boiling juice.

8. Stir the juice and sugar mixture until it returns to a full boil and until all the sugar dissolves. Once the sugar dissolves, continue boiling for 1 minute more.

9. Remove the syrup from the heat, ladle it into the canning jars, apply the lids and bands, and process the jars fully submerged in boiling water for 10 minutes. (Refer to steps 12 through 17 on page 150 of the "Making Classic Cooked Jam or Jelly" section for specifics.)

Sugaring

Mixology

A lot of mixed drinks rely on simple syrup as the sweetener, while others use liqueurs both to sweeten drinks and add flavor. Your homemade fruit syrups can take the place of liqueurs in fruity drinks.

If you're not interested in fruity mixed drinks, perhaps you enjoy wine and beer coolers. Homemade fruit syrups are perfect for sweetening these drinks. Add cherry or raspberry syrup to sangria, for example, or to beer, to create satisfying new flavors. Here's a recipe to try for sangria:

1 (750-ml) bottle Merlot or Cabernet Sauvignon wine

½ cup raspberry syrup

2 cups water or club soda

2 lemons

2 limes

4 oranges

Chill the wine, syrup, and water or soda. Juice 1 lemon, 1 lime, and 3 oranges and slice the remaining fruits in round sections. Remove the seeds and put the juice and fruit slices into a large pitcher. Add the wine, syrup, and water or soda and serve over ice, or neat.

Black Raspberry Teriyaki

Calling this "teriyaki" is a bit of a stretch because raspberry syrup overwhelms the distinct flavor of teriyaki marinade. Still, my family is enthusiastic about the results when I marinate chicken or beef in this mixture and grill it.

Makes 4 to 10 servings

Up to 7 boneless, skinless chicken breast halves or up to 3 pounds London broil

1/3 cup soy sauce

1/3 cup dry sherry or cooking wine

1/3 cup black raspberry syrup

2 teaspoons grated fresh ginger

1 small onion, peeled and diced

1/4 teaspoon salt

1/4 teaspoon ground black pepper

Prepare the chicken or beef for marinating. If the meat can marinate for 6 or more hours, you can leave the chicken breasts or London broil whole, if desired. Or, and this is my preference, cut the chicken into 1/4- to 1/2-inch strips before marinating; cut the beef into 1/8-inch strips.

Combine the remaining ingredients in a zipper-top bag, zip the bag shut, and massage it to mix the ingredients well. Open the bag and add the meat to marinate. Zip the bag nearly shut, fold it over, squeeze out as much air as possible until the marinade nearly reaches the top of the bag, and finish zipping it shut. Set the bag in the refrigerator for up to 8 hours before grilling.

For whole chicken breasts, grill on high heat for 6 to 9 minutes on each side. Grill a whole London broil on high heat for 9 to 12 minutes on each side. Let the London broil rest for 10 minutes after grilling, then slice it into 1/8-inch strips across the grain for serving.

If you've marinated chicken or beef strips, mount them on bamboo spears before grilling and sear them for 2 to 3 minutes on high heat on each side.

Sugaring

Candied Fruits

The craft of candying fruits seems to have gone the way of the dodo bird. My grandmother occasionally served a platter of candied lemon and orange rind, but outside of my own kitchen I've seen no one candying fruits of any kind.

I encourage you to have a go at it. Fruits you candy at home will be unlike any other confection you're likely to experience. The best description I can offer is that it has some of the character of gummy candies, but with the flavor of actual fruit. A bowl or bag of candied fruits could satisfy any fan of gumdrops and gummy bears.

Is there a compelling culinary use for candied fruit? Fruitcake? Maybe that's not such a crazy idea. Fruits you candy at home are tastier than the candied fruits you can buy in a grocery store, and a homemade fruitcake containing them will put most commercial fruitcakes to shame (which isn't hard to do anyway). Candied fruits make great garnishes for fruit-flavored cakes and pastries, and for ice cream desserts such as sundaes and cakes.

Make Fruity Candies

There are many methods for making candied fruit, but reject any that claim you can succeed by cooking fruit once in a bath of simple syrup. Your goal is to force the fruit to absorb so much sugar that it completely alters the texture of the fruit, and cooking it once in syrup simply won't do the job.

NOTE

I've seen a recipe that involves starting the fruit in simple syrup and cooking it slowly for several hours until the syrup has all but evaporated. This method sounds workable, but I'm one of those people who would forget the candy was cooking and end up with a pot of charred fruit.

Some fruits won't survive the candying procedure. Among the best for candying are cherries and pineapple. Rinds of citrus fruits were historically very popular for candying, and you'll do okay with peaches, pears, plums, very firm apples, and mangoes. I've had great luck with cantaloupe and have heard that watermelon also candies very well.

Making Candied Fruit

1. Rinse, peel, core, pit, or otherwise prepare 1 cup or less of fruit. Cut the fruit into 1-inch square pieces, though larger pieces will work (whole pitted cherries are fine). To candy citrus rinds, follow the instructions in "Prepare Citrus Rinds for Candying" on page 174.

2. Make simple syrup in a small to medium-sized saucepan. To do this, mix 1 cup sugar with 1 cup water in the pot and bring it to a boil.

3. While the syrup is boiling, add the fruit or citrus rinds and let the mixture return to a boil.

4. Immediately lower the heat so the mixture simmers; it needn't boil, but if you can't get the heat low enough to stop it, that's okay. Simmer for 20 minutes.

5. Remove the pot from the stove and let the syrup and fruit cool to room temperature. I usually leave it overnight.

6. Separate the fruit from the syrup and return the syrup to the stove. Heat the syrup, and add another cup of sugar, and bring to a boil until the sugar dissolves.

7. Add the fruit back to the boiling syrup, let the syrup return to a boil, then lower the heat and simmer again for 20 minutes.

8. Remove the pot from the stove and let the syrup and fruit cool to room temperature. I usually leave it overnight. (Does this seem familiar?)

9. Separate the fruit from the syrup—this may not be so easy as sometimes the syrup thickens and "locks in" the fruit. So if necessary, return the syrup and fruit to the stove and heat the mixture until it's liquid enough to remove the fruit. Then heat just the syrup, add another 1 cup sugar, and bring to a boil until the sugar dissolves.

10. Add the fruit back to the boiling syrup, let the syrup return to a boil, then lower the heat and simmer one final time for 20 minutes. At this point, you may be feeling a sense of déjà vu.

11. Fish the fruit out of the syrup and distribute it on a cooling rack with a plate, pan, or paper underneath the rack to catch the drips. The fruit will be translucent and very sticky.

12. After several hours or even on the next day, roll the fruit pieces in sugar. You can wrap the candied fruit in wax paper or leave it out to dry further; it may take several days to harden,

but you can shorten the drying time by placing the cooling racks in a warm oven or by transferring the candies to a dedicated food dehydrator.

From the Tip Jar

Use the concentrated syrup left over from candying fruit to sweeten and flavor drinks such as limeade, lemonade, and sangria. Or if you're an experienced candy maker, you can probably devise taffies and hard candies using the syrup as a base.

Sugaring

Prepare Citrus Rinds for Candying

Candied citrus rinds are delicious, but they require a bit more preparation than other fruits do. For oranges, limes, lemons, and grapefruits, prepare rinds as follows before putting them through the sugaring procedures that begin with Step 2 in the preceding procedure for making fruity candies.

1. Wash the fruit and cut it into segments—quarters for smaller fruits, eighths for larger.

2. Remove the fruit from the rind (eat the fruit, make fruit salad, or whatever) and scrape the insides of the peels down to the soft white material called the "pith."

3. Especially with grapefruit, pith can impart a bitter flavor in the finished candy. So use a sharp knife to cut the pith off of the rind and discard the pith. Alternatively, you can get thicker pieces of candy if you leave the pith on the rind and cook the bitterness out of the pith by blanching the rind two or three times in succession: cover the rinds with cold water, bring to a boil, and then pour off the hot water.

4. Slice the citrus peel into strips or wedges, depending on your preference.

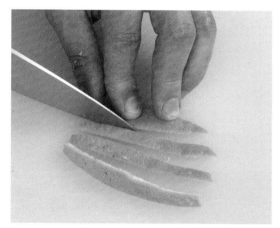

Candied Vegetables?

Yes, you can candy vegetables, and in some cases, it's even worth doing. You might have experience with candied carrots as they sometimes garnish carrot cakes. Many root vegetables candy quite well, though they tend to be firmer than candied fruits.

It's hard to predict whether you'll want to eat a particular candied vegetable. I believe candied ginger is way too strong for most people to consume as snack food, but if you enjoy Asian cooking, you might occasionally need candied ginger for some of your recipes. Being a great fan of onions, I once candied onion segments. They came out beautifully, but they didn't win me over. Still, I imagine they'd taste great diced and added to a sweet-and-sour wilted spinach salad.

Finally, consider potatoes as a blank canvas for candied vegetable creations. Having a mild flavor, potatoes will absorb whatever flavoring you add to the syrup in which you candy them. Cook mint leaves in the simple syrup before you add cooked potato strips or add peppermint extract to the cooking syrup. Try such flavors as vanilla, root beer, or lemon extract. Make honey-flavored candies by swapping ¼ cup honey for ¼ cup sugar when you first make the syrup.

From the Tip Jar

When candying vegetables such as carrots and potatoes, cut thin slices— ⅛ inch or thinner—and cook them until they're just done; don't let them get soft enough to break apart easily. When you candy vegetables, add a generous number of apple slices to the syrup along with the vegetable slices. The apples release pectin into the syrup, which decreases its tendency to crystallize when cooking and cooling, and you also end up with delicious apple candy along with your candied vegetables.

Your Sugar High

I hope you'll try your hand at sugaring. At least make jam or jelly. If your family doesn't eat it, you know people who will. Give homemade preserves as gifts and people will react as if you've mastered alchemy. But once you've made a few batches of jam and jelly, you'll appreciate how easy it is to do. If you don't tell anyone, I won't either, and you can continue to wow friends and family with your amazing skill.

Chapter 7

Canning Low-Acid Foods

Pressure canning is easy. I want to get that out quickly to encourage you to stay with me in this chapter. Really, pressure canning is no harder than the boiling water bath canning you use to preserve high-acid foods such as fruits, tomato products, pickles, relishes, jams, and jellies. The significant difference is that you must have a special canning pot for pressure canning.

For the most part, foods preserved under pressure have decent texture and flavor, resembling fresh-cooked vegetables. In fact, some canning enthusiasts feel that nearly everything you can under pressure is better than the same product canned in a boiling water bath canner.

Pressure Cooking Miracles

If you're getting a pot for pressure canning, it could easily earn your respect as a versatile cooking appliance as well. Pressure cooking is like putting food into a slow cooker and taking it out fully cooked after one-tenth or less of the normal cooking time.

So, for example, a pot roast that might cook in your slow cooker for 8 to 10 hours could emerge from your pressure cooker in just 45 minutes and have all the same characteristics of a slow-cooked pot roast. A 6-pound pork roast will cook in 1 hour, while three whole chickens together will cook in 10 minutes!

My pressure canner has saved me on days when I've forgotten to thaw a roast so it would be ready for the oven in the late afternoon. The pressure canner (as cooker) can take a 3-pound roast from frozen to serving in about 90 minutes.

A pressure canner will come with instructions for pressure cooking and usually several recipes to get you started. With a little research, you'll find instructions for cooking nearly every cut of meat, main courses, casseroles, and even desserts in your pressure canner.

Canning Low-Acid Foods

The whole point of pressure canning is to kill a specific microbe that considers boiling water merely to be a comfortable temperature. This microbe, Clostridium botulinum, is present on virtually all food, but it requires very specific conditions before it can do harm: it must find its way into a moist, low-acid, oxygen-free environment.

Canning high-acid foods creates a moist, oxygen-free environment, but the acidic conditions keep Clostridium in check. Without acid, your canning procedure must completely kill Clostridium. Pressure canning succeeds by raising the temperature of preserved food to 240 degrees Fahrenheit—a temperature deadly even to Clostridium.

Actually, the cooking times I cite for pressure cooking on page 177 are a bit optimistic. They represent how long the canner must remain at full pressure. So add 20 to 30 minutes to the stated cooking times to account for heating and cooling the pressure canner.

What Can You Can Under Pressure?

Pressure canning will kill Clostridium in fruits, vegetables, meat, and poultry; that's right, you can preserve meat by canning. The United States Department of Agriculture (USDA) publishes guidelines for preparation of food and duration of processing under pressure for all kinds of fruits, vegetables, meats, and prepared foods such as soups and pie fillings.

The USDA discourages canning of some products—ones that are very dense or that contain flour or cornstarch. Densely packed foods such as mashed or strained vegetables don't heat through reliably, and flour and cornstarch break down enough during canning that the USDA recommends home canners shouldn't use them.

Because a boiling water bath canner does such a great job of preserving fruits and other high-acid foods, this chapter examines only low-acid foods with an emphasis on vegetables. The USDA guidelines are specific, and there's no room for creativity; follow the guidelines faithfully to ensure your canned goods remain nontoxic.

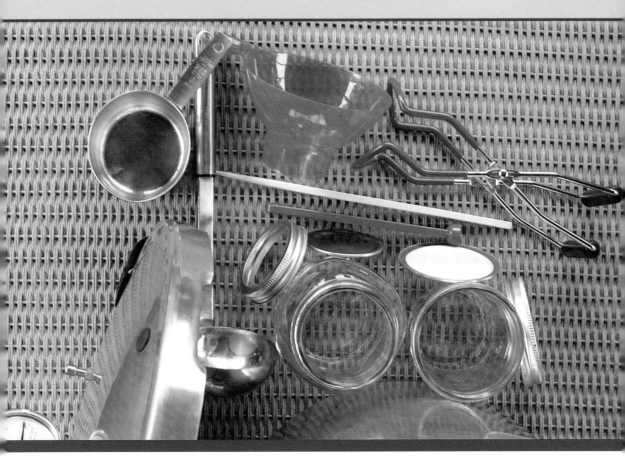

Equipment for Pressure Canning

The equipment you use for boiling water bath canning is also useful for pressure canning with the obvious exception of the canning pot. A brief description, an explanation, and a photo of each item appears in Chapter 5 beginning on page 108. Here are items that are useful for pressure canning:

- Assorted knives, a vegetable peeler, spoons, bowls, and saucepans

- Canning jars, lids, and bands

- Jar lifter

- Canning funnel

- Lid lifter

- Band tightener (lid wrench)

- Bubble releaser

- Ladle

- Pressure canning pot

- Canning rack (This should come with the canning pot; it's usually a metal disk that rests on the bottom and provides a small gap between the jars and the pot's bottom.)

Canning Low-Acid Foods

The Pressure Canner

At sea level, water boils at 212 degrees Fahrenheit. When you pressurize water, you increase the temperature at which it boils. A pressure canner does exactly that: the lid locks onto the rim of the pot, making an airtight seal. When ten pounds of pressure develops inside the pot, the water boils at a temperature of 240 degrees Fahrenheit.

If that's all there was to a pressure canner, there wouldn't be many canning enthusiasts. Cooking a sealed container will likely cause it to explode. As you would expect, a pressure canner has features to prevent explosions.

• Every pressure canner has some type of fail-safe vent or "overpressure release plug." This is a valve or a "cork" in the lid that opens automatically to relieve pressure if it builds up beyond the maximum level required for cooking.

• Every pressure canner has a vent pipe through which steam flows while the canner is hot and under pressure. Unless you seriously overheat a pressure canner, the vent pipe is adequate to keep it from ever building up an unsafe amount of pressure.

There are two basic designs for home pressure canners: weighted-gauge canners and dial-gauge canners. A third, less common design uses an adjustable switch to choose between two pressure settings.

Weighted-gauge canners. The pressure canner with the simplest design uses a set of weights to control pressure inside the canning pot. You put a weight, or a combination of weights, on the pot's vent pipe, and pressurized steam lifts the weight up on its way out of the pot. The weights that come with your canning pot may combine to create 5 pounds of cooking pressure, 10 pounds of pressure, and 15 pounds. One design uses a single weight, and the way you position it during canning determines how much pressure develops in the pot.

Dial-gauge canners. With a dial-gauge canner, a numbered dial reveals the actual pressure inside the canner. By monitoring this gauge, you can hold the pressure very precisely, anywhere from just a few pounds up to 15 pounds. Even with a dial gauge, a pressure canner comes with a weight to put on the vent pipe. This weight will hold the canner at 15 pounds of pressure and acts as a safety valve should you have trouble controlling the pressure yourself.

Pick Your Gauge

For the most part, people are happy with either type of gauge. Some canners, though, work only at 15 pounds of pressure—far more than is necessary to make your food safe.

Remember that canning cooks food. If you cook vegetables under unnecessarily high pressure, they'll end up mushy. So when you shop for a weighted-gauge pressure canner, make sure it can maintain pressure at several levels—5, 10, and 15 pounds are common, with 10 pounds being appropriate for canning.

A dial-gauge canner gives you nearly pinpoint control over the pressure inside the canner. Simply by adjusting the heat setting on your stove, you can set and hold the pressure as needed for canning.

Pressure canners come in many sizes, with the most versatile being the largest. A canner that can hold seven quart-sized jars can also hold nine pint jars. Better still, manufacturers usually make 9-quart pressure canners deep enough that they'll accommodate two layers of pint jars. This means you can process as many as eighteen pint jars of produce at once when you're cooking them under pressure. If your canning needs are great, you can find pressure canners to handle fourteen quart jars and even nineteen quarts at once, but keep in mind that those things are really heavy.

A full-sized 9-quart pressure canner can double as a boiling water bath canner. One great advantage of this is that you need only one pot to handle both types of canning. You can't stack jars for boiling water bath canning, but that limitation exists whatever the design of your canning pot.

Care of Your Canner

Read your pressure canner's instruction booklet! It may contain product-specific information that is critical to your safety and to proper maintenance of the canner. Certain cautions need emphasis:

• Read and understand how to operate the pressure canner before you start. I promise it's easy, but don't let its ease of use make you careless.

• Make sure the canner's vent pipe has nothing in it. You should be able to see light through it.

• The pressure canner gets really hot during canning, so don't touch the metal surfaces. (Was this too obvious to mention?)

• Avoid contact with steam or vapor coming from the pressure canner.

• Don't use a pressure canner as cookware in an oven.

• Don't try to open a pressure canner when it's under pressure. The instructions that come with a canning pot will explain how to recognize when its contents are no longer under pressure.

• Don't use a pressure canner on a burner or range that can deliver more than 12,000 BTUs. Burners intended for deep-frying turkeys may be too hot for pressure canning.

• Follow the manufacturer's maintenance schedule for replacing components of your pressure canner. If you're not sure whether you're on the recommended schedule, replace any serviceable rubber parts—usually a gasket that fits between the lid and the rim of the pot, and the overpressure plug that pops out of the lid if pressure in the canner becomes too great. If you see any damage or wear on either of these components, replace them.

• If you have a dial-gauge pressure canner, take the gauge to your local Cooperative Extension office annually for testing. (The Cooperative Extension Service is a nationwide educational network affiliated with the USDA.) Alternatively, check with your canner's manufacturer, which may provide a testing service if you mail in the gauge.

• Always use the lowest possible heat setting on your stove that maintains the proper pressure in your canner. If you drive the canner hard, it may lose moisture too quickly, resulting in damaged canned goods.

• Use your pressure canner only on a level burner. The various pressure regulators on the canner may not work properly if the canner isn't level.

• Don't use a pressure canner on a stove that has a flat glass cooktop. A pressure canner full of produce may be heavy enough to crack the glass.

When the Canner Cools

Your pressure canner's lid may have a built-in air vent whose default position is "open." In that position, the vent appears as a metal disk recessed within a socket in the lid. When adequate pressure builds up in the canning pot, the pressure pushes the vent closed; the disk rises above the lid, providing an obvious indication that the pot holds pressure.

On my pressure canner, this air vent doubles as a cover lock; when the vent closes (rises), it locks the lid in place so I couldn't possibly force it open. Before you fill your canning pot and set it on the heat, make sure the air vent on your lid can move freely. One simple way to do this is to turn the lid upside down and check whether the cylinder drops down from its socket.

As the canning pot cools, it continues to blow steam through the vent pipe until there is no more pressure in the pot. At that point, the air vent drops back into its socket; the canning pot is ready to open.

Steps for Pressure Canning

It's time to see just how easy pressure canning is. The steps are remarkably similar to those of boiling water bath canning. Procedures are identical for every pressure canning project, though they vary slightly depending on the design of your canning pot. I can't provide specifics for every type of pressure canner, so I must emphasize that you should read and follow the manufacturer's instructions. Here are the steps to pressure canning vegetables:

1. Inspect your pressure canner for wear. Don't use it if the gaskets are torn or appear worn, stretched, or hardened.

2. Examine your canning jars and reject any that have cracks or chips. Select clean, rust-free bands and use only new canning lids. Fill the canning jars with hot water and put the canning lids in a pot of water on low heat; don't set the stove's heat high enough to boil the water.

From the Tip Jar

After filling jars with hot water, I place them in my pressure canner to keep them out of the way. This is a challenge when canning two layers of pint-sized or smaller jars.

3. Prepare liquid and produce for canning. For most produce you can raw pack or hot pack the jars (see the box on page 184). Refer to the "Produce-Specific Procedures" section on page 187 to help you decide which method you'll use. Also, heat the water you'll need to generate steam in your pressure canner; it will need to be boiling when you've finished packing the jars.

Raw Pack or Hot Pack?

When you raw pack vegetables, you cut them into appropriate sizes and put them directly into canning jars. Then you pour boiling hot canning liquid (usually water) into the jars, apply lids and bands, and put the jars into the canning pot.

In a hot pack, you dump the prepared vegetables into boiling canning fluid (again, usually water) and cook them for several minutes. Then you fish the vegetables out of the canning fluid, pack them into canning jars, and top up the jars with the hot fluid. As with a raw pack, you apply lids and bands and set the jars in the canning pot.

Refer to the "Produce-Specific Procedures" section on page 187 for guidelines about raw- and hot-packing vegetables.

4. Empty the hot canning jars and fill them with produce and hot canning liquid. Work a chopstick, a bamboo skewer, or a dedicated bubble releaser down the insides of the jars to release the air bubbles. Use all the vegetables, leaving 1 inch of headspace in each jar.

5. Apply a lid to each jar and screw on a band, tightening it "finger tight." By that, I mean give it a good, hard twist, but not as though you're trying to twist off the neck of the canning jar.

6. Put your canning pot on the burner and pour boiling water into it. Each canning pot has its own requirements for the volume of water to add, so look for this information in the instructions that came with the canner. If you can't find a reference, use enough water to fill the canning pot 1½ inches deep; with pressure canning, you don't submerge the jars in water. Add the canning rack and place the jars on it. Don't process jars in your canner without using the rack.

From the Tip Jar

Supposedly, you'll prevent water stains on the sides of your canning jars if you add a few tablespoons of white vinegar to the water. In my experience, you still might get water stains or you might not.

7. Make a final inspection of the canning pot's lid: is the vent pipe clear? Then lock the lid onto the canning pot. Some canners have interlocking flanges that you engage by rotating the lid onto the pot. Others have thumbscrews that you tighten to lock the lid down onto the flat rim of the canning pot. Follow the instructions that came with your canner.

8. Turn the burner on high and wait for steam to blow hard from the canning pot's vent pipe, then turn the heat down but not enough to diminish the steam. Let the steam continue to blow for 10 minutes.

9. Place the pressure-regulating weight on the vent pipe. Careful! Don't test the steam with your skin. If you're using a weighted-gauge canner, use the 10-pound weight combination or setting. If you're using a dial-gauge canner, there should be only one weight (which lets the canner build up to 15 pounds of pressure).

10. Let the pressure build. For dial gauges, monitor the gauge until it shows the target pressure, usually 11 pounds, then adjust the heat on the burner to hold the pressure there. You'll use a surprisingly low setting to maintain the correct pressure. For weighted gauges, listen for the pressure-regulating weight to chatter. When the canner's pressure is high enough, steam will momentarily displace the weight, releasing just a little pressure and causing the weight to click. On high heat, this will happen dozens of times a minute, causing the weight to chatter or stutter; it's okay to turn the heat down as long as the weight continues to click three or four times per minute.

Start timing when your canner reaches the correct pressure.

11. If the pressure in the canner drops below the prescribed level even briefly during cooking, increase the heat of the burner until the pressure increases appropriately. Then begin timing again from the start; failure to maintain pressure for the entire time may result in your produce spoiling. At the end of the processing time, turn off the stove and remove the canner from the burner.

WARNING!

Don't try to speed the cooling of the pressure canner; if it cools down too quickly, the canning jars inside of it could break, or worse, the canner itself could crack.

12. Let the canner cool, which may take 20 to 45 minutes; don't rush it. If your canner has an air valve, wait for it to drop back into its socket. You can also test by wobbling the pressure regulator weight on the vent pipe; if no steam emerges, the pressure is down. Remove the weight from the vent pipe and let the canner continue to cool for 10 more minutes.

13. Open the canner cautiously. Either rotate the lid or remove the thumbscrews. When you lift the lid, tilt the far side of it up, keeping the rest of the lid between you and the mouth of the canning pot.

14. Remove the jars from the canner without tilting them and set them on a cooling rack or on a towel spread on the counter. Let them cool to room temperature.

Competition Canning

Canning long ago inspired enthusiasts to pit their preserved vegetables against each other. You can witness these battles throughout the summer at county and state fairs all over the United States.

Combatants complete their canning projects and fill out an entry form, which they submit with an entry fee (in some cases). Then they deliver a jar of produce to the fairground where it will compete. Rules usually forbid spectators to be present when judges are examining the jars and selecting winners.

After being judged, the canned goods go on display along with the ribbons they've won. Then, for the rest of the fair, visitors can walk through and admire the goodies. I'm always fascinated by the shelves of canned goods at county fairs. It warms my heart to know that people have such passion for preserving produce.

15. Test the lids; they should bow down into the jars. To be sure they're tight, remove the bands and lift each jar by the edges of its lid. If any haven't sealed, reprocess the jar using a new canning lid, or store the jar in your refrigerator and use it within a week.

16. Label your jars with the contents and the date and store them in a cool, dry place. Don't leave the bands on the jars during storage; they tend to rust and stick, sometimes becoming very difficult to remove.

Produce-Specific Procedures

If you're canning vegetables and you don't want to ferment or quick pickle them first, then you must use a pressure canner. You'll have best results from canning vegetables on the day you harvest them. Actually, because of the harsh cooking that takes place during canning, many people prefer produce to be just a bit underripe; don't can anything that's overripe.

To prepare vegetables for canning, prep them as you would for cooking. Then choose from the two methods of packing jars, raw pack or hot pack.

For both raw-packed and hot-packed vegetables, leave 1 inch of headspace. Then apply lids and bands, and set the jars in the canning pot.

Asparagus

Harvest/Buy: You'll need 25 pounds to fill 7 quart jars, or 16 pounds to fill 9 pint jars.

Select: Choose young shoots whose buds are tight and whose leaf scales are flat against the stems.

Prepare: Wash and trim the asparagus. There's a trick to finding the right amount to trim from an asparagus stalk: hold the tip end in one hand and the cut end in the other. Bend the asparagus spear until it snaps and discard the cut-end section. Leave spears whole or cut them into pieces.

Can: To raw pack asparagus, pack the vegetables tightly in canning jars and add boiling water, leaving 1 inch of headspace. To hot pack, add the asparagus to boiling water. When it returns to a boil, cook for 2 to 3 minutes. Fish the asparagus out and loosely pack it into canning jars. Add the boiling cooking water to cover, leaving 1 inch of headspace. Release air bubbles, add lids and bands, and process according to the "Low-Acid Foods Pressure and Timing" table on page 195, adjusting for altitude, if necessary.

Beans (Green, Snap, Wax)

Harvest/Buy: You'll need 14 pounds to fill 7 quart jars, or 9 pounds to fill 9 pint jars.

Select: Choose tender, ripe pods that haven't developed mature beans. Reject pods that are soft, shriveled, or displaying disease.

Prepare: Wash the beans and snap off and discard the ends. Leave beans whole or snap them into bite-sized lengths.

Can: To raw pack beans, fill canning jars tightly with raw beans and add boiling water, leaving 1 inch of headspace. To hot pack, add raw beans to boiling water and when it returns to a boil, cook for 5 minutes. Fish the beans out of the water and loosely pack them into canning jars. Add the boiling cooking water, leaving 1 inch of headspace. Release air bubbles, add lids and bands, and process according to the "Low-Acid Foods Pressure and Timing" table on page 195, adjusting for altitude, if necessary.

Beets

Harvest/Buy: You'll need 21 pounds to fill 7 quart jars, or 14 pounds to fill 9 pint jars.

Select: Use tender, young roots less than 3 inches wide. Reject beets that show insect damage or evidence of spoilage.

Prepare: Wash the beets well and trim stems and roots so 1 inch of each remains. Add the beets to boiling water and when it returns to a boil, cook for 15 to 25 minutes. The skins should slip off easily; remove the skins and cut off the stems and roots. Leave small beets whole, if you wish, and cut larger beets into bite-sized pieces.

Beets retain color better if you cook them whole with their stems and roots on. Don't cut them up until after the initial 15 to 25 minutes of boiling.

Can: Pack the hot beets loosely into canning jars and add the boiling cooking water, leaving 1 inch of headspace. Release air bubbles, add lids and bands, and process according to the "Low-Acid Foods Pressure and Timing" table on page 195, adjusting for altitude, if necessary.

From the Tip Jar

When you hot pack produce, you cook it at least a little bit before packing it in canning jars. Try to work quickly; produce you leave in the water will continue to cook, and you'll have variation between vegetables from the time you begin packing and when you end.

I use a strainer to scoop produce out of the cooking fluid and transfer it into a large bowl. I leave the cooking fluid on the burner so it stays hot while I pack jars with produce from the bowl.

Carrots

Harvest/Buy: You'll need 18 pounds (without tops) to fill 7 quart jars, or 11 pounds to fill 9 pint jars.

Select: Choose crisp, tender carrots that you would prepare for a meal. Harvest before the carrots produce a flower stalk. Cut away sections that have insect damage or that show signs of spoilage.

Prepare: Wash the carrots well, peel them, cut away the top ¼ inch (to remove the bitter carrot shoulders), and wash them again. Leave carrots whole or cut them into shapes you prefer—spears, chunks, or slices are fine.

Can: To raw pack, fill canning jars tightly with raw carrots and add boiling water, leaving 1 inch of headspace. To hot pack, add raw carrots to boiling water and when it returns to a boil, cook for 5 minutes. Fish the carrots out of the water and pack them into canning jars. Add the boiling cooking water, leaving 1 inch of headspace. Release air bubbles, add lids and bands, and process according to the "Low-Acid Foods Pressure and Timing" table on page 195, adjusting for altitude, if necessary.

Corn

Harvest/Buy: You'll need 1 bushel of corn on the cob to fill 7 quart jars. Two-thirds of a bushel will fill 9 pint jars.

Select: Choose fresh, young sweet corn that you'd be happy to eat fresh; don't can mature, tough, or starchy corn.

Prepare: Remove the husks and corn silk, and then wash the corn. Blanch for 3 minutes in boiling water. Cut the kernels off of the cob at three-fourths the depth of the kernels. If you cut too deeply, you'll get corn cob in the mix, which makes for very unpleasant chewing.

Can: To raw pack, fill jars loosely with corn and add boiling water, leaving 1 inch of headspace. To hot pack, measure the corn kernels as you transfer them to a large pot. Add 1 cup water for each quart of corn, bring to a boil, and cook for 5 minutes. Fish the corn out of the water and fill canning jars, leaving 1 inch of headspace. Then add the boiling cooking water, again leaving 1 inch of headspace. Release air bubbles, add lids and bands, and process according to the "Low-Acid Foods Pressure and Timing" table on page 195, adjusting for altitude, if necessary.

Canning Low-Acid Foods

Greens (Beets, Collards, Kale, Mustard, Spinach, Swiss Chard)

Harvest/Buy: You'll need 28 pounds to fill 7 quart jars, or 18 pounds to fill 9 pints.

Select: Use young, perfect leaves. Reject any that are tough, fibrous, wilted, discolored, or chewed by insects.

Prepare: Wash the greens by floating them in cold water and gently agitating them so any soil sinks to the bottom of the container. Pick through the leaves, removing critters and gently wiping away stuck-on dirt. Remove thick stems and veins from the leaves. Heat the water you'll add to jars when you pack the greens.

Can: Steam blanch the greens for 3 to 5 minutes, about 1 pound of leaves at a time. Place them loosely into canning jars and add the boiling water, leaving 1 inch of headspace. Release air bubbles, add lids and bands, and process according to the "Low-Acid Foods Pressure and Timing" table on page 195, adjusting for altitude, if necessary.

Lima Beans

Harvest/Buy: You'll need 28 pounds to fill 7 quart jars, or 18 pounds to fill 9 pint jars.

Select: Choose full pods with seeds of appropriate color. Reject any lima beans you wouldn't want to eat.

Prepare: Shell and wash the lima beans.

Can: To raw pack lima beans, fill canning jars loosely with raw beans and add boiling water, leaving headspace as follows:

Pints: 1 inch

Quarts of small lima beans: 1½ inches

Quarts of large lima beans: 1¼ inches

To hot pack, add raw beans to boiling water. When it returns to a boil, cook for 3 minutes. Fish the beans out of the water and loosely pack them into canning jars. Add the boiling cooking water, leaving 1 inch of headspace. Release air bubbles, add lids and bands, and process according to the "Low-Acid Foods Pressure and Timing" table on page 195, adjusting for altitude, if necessary.

Okra

Harvest/Buy: You'll need 11 pounds to fill 7 quart jars, or 7 pounds to fill 9 pints.

Select: Pick young, tender okra pods, rejecting any that are shriveled or diseased.

Prepare: Wash the okra, remove the stems, and trim the ends. Leave the pods whole or slice them into 1-inch sections. Place the prepared okra in a large pot, cover it with hot water, and bring the water to a boil. Cook for 2 minutes.

Can: Remove the lightly cooked okra from the boiling water and pack it into canning jars, leaving 1 inch of headspace. Fill the jars with the boiling cooking water, again leaving 1 inch of headspace. Release air bubbles, add lids and bands, and process according to the "Low-Acid Foods Pressure and Timing" table on page 195, adjusting for altitude, if necessary.

Peas (Shelled)

Harvest/Buy: You'll need 32 pounds to fill 7 quart jars, or 20 pounds to fill 9 pint jars.

Select: Choose pods that are plump without being crowded; reject peas that are hard, starchy, or diseased.

Prepare: Shell and rinse the peas.

Can: To raw pack peas, fill jars with raw peas. Add boiling water, leaving 1 inch of headspace. To hot pack, add raw peas to boiling water. When the water returns to a boil, cook for 2 minutes. Fish the peas out of the water and put them in jars. Add the boiling cooking water, leaving 1 inch of headspace. Release air bubbles, add lids and bands, and process according to the "Low-Acid Foods Pressure and Timing" table on page 195, adjusting for altitude, if necessary.

Peppers (All Types)

Harvest/Buy: You'll need 9 pounds to fill 9 pint jars. The USDA doesn't publish guidelines for canning peppers in quart jars.

Select: Choose green or fully ripe peppers, rejecting any that are soft or discolored or that appear diseased.

Roasted Peppers Reduce Heartburn

Many people report that eating peppers (sweet or hot) gives them heartburn. Don't let this stop you from enjoying them in cooking. It's usually the outer skin of the pepper that causes gastronomical distress. Roast the peppers and remove their skins and there's a reasonable chance you can eat peppers without problems.

There are several ways to roast peppers for canning:

Oven. Heat the oven to 400 degrees Fahrenheit. Bake whole peppers for 6 to 8 minutes.

Broiler. Adjust the broiling rack so the sides of the peppers are about 3 inches from the heating element. Watch the roasting peppers and turn them once when the skins begin to darken. Remove them when the skins have cooked on both sides. It's okay if there are charred spots on the peppers.

Stovetop. Cover a burner with a cooking rack such as one from a barbecue grill—or use a dedicated chili pepper roasting rack available from many cooking stores—and turn the burner to high. Roast peppers until the skins blister, turning them as needed to cook the skins all around. It's okay if the peppers get just a little charred. Whichever way you roast peppers, let them cool, cover them for 5 minutes with a damp towel, and then peel off the skins.

Prepare: Blanch whole peppers in boiling water for 3 minutes. Or roast the peppers and remove their skins as directed in the "Roasted Peppers Reduce Heartburn" box on the left. Whether you blanch or roast the peppers, remove the stems and seeds and cut the peppers into sections (there's no need to cut up small peppers).

Can: Pack the prepared peppers loosely in canning jars and add the boiling cooking water, leaving 1 inch of headspace. Release air bubbles, add lids and bands, and process according to the "Low-Acid Foods Pressure and Timing" table on page 195, adjusting for altitude, if necessary.

Potatoes

Harvest/Buy: You'll need 20 pounds to fill 7 quart jars, or 13 pounds to fill 9 pint jars.

Select: Choose potatoes that are ready to eat. Reject soft potatoes or any whose eyes have begun to sprout. Remove green or discolored potato flesh. Potatoes that have been in cold storage may change color if you can them.

Prepare: If you wish to can small new potatoes (1 to 2½ inches wide) whole in their skins, wash them, brush them, and rinse them to remove all soil. Or for potatoes of any size, wash and peel them and cut them into ½-inch cubes. While you're working, float the prepared pieces in ascorbic acid solution consisting of 1 teaspoon ascorbic acid powder dissolved in 1 gallon water (read about ascorbic acid in Chapter 5 on page 120). Place the prepared potatoes in a large pot, cover them with hot water, and bring to a boil. Once they're boiling, cook whole potatoes for 10 minutes or cubed potatoes for 2 minutes, and drain.

Can: Pack canning jars with potatoes or potato pieces, then fill the jars with fresh boiling water (don't use the water in which you originally blanched the potatoes), leaving 1 inch of headspace. Release air bubbles, add lids and bands, and process according to the "Low-Acid Foods Pressure and Timing" table on page 195, adjusting for altitude, if necessary.

Winter Squash and Pumpkins

Harvest/Buy: You'll need 16 pounds to fill 7 quart jars, or 10 pounds to fill 9 pint jars.

Select: Choose ripe squash or pumpkins that have firm skin and no soft spots. If you're canning pumpkin, choose varieties specifically intended for cooking; other varieties may have stringy flesh and contain less sugar.

WARNING!

Don't mash squash or pumpkins before canning, and don't force the prepared produce into canning jars. The USDA has not identified a safe home-canning method for mashed pumpkins and squash.

Prepare: Wash, peel, seed, and cut up the squash or pumpkins into 1-inch cubes. Bring water to a boil in a large pot and add the pumpkin or squash cubes. When the water resumes boiling, cook the pumpkin or squash for 2 minutes.

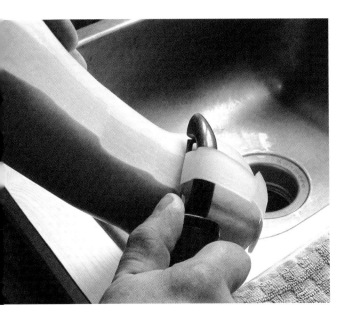

I find it easiest to peel smooth-skinned squashes such as butternut by using a vegetable peeler. Hold the whole fruit down on the counter and make strokes with the peeler away from your body.

Can: Fish the cubes out of the water and pack them in canning jars. Add the boiling cooking water to cover the cubes, leaving 1 inch of headspace. Release air bubbles, add lids and bands, and process according to the "Low-Acid Foods Pressure and Timing" table on page 195, adjusting for altitude, if necessary.

Yams (Sweet Potatoes)

Harvest/Buy: You'll need 18 pounds to fill 7 quart jars, or 11 pounds to fill 9 pint jars.

Select: Choose yams that are ready to eat. Reject soft yams or any that have become stringy.

Prepare: Wash the yams, peel them, cut them into uniform bite-sized pieces, and cook them in boiling water or steam them until they start to soften, 7 to 10 minutes, depending on the size of the pieces you prepared.

Can: Strain the yam pieces and discard the boiling water. Then pack the yams loosely in canning jars. Add fresh boiling water to the jars, leaving 1 inch of headspace. Release air bubbles, add lids and bands, and process according to the "Low-Acid Foods Pressure and Timing" table on page 195, adjusting for altitude, if necessary.

WARNING!

Don't mash yams before canning, or compress them into the canning jars. The mashed produce is too dense to process safely in a home pressure canner.

LOW-ACID FOODS PRESSURE AND TIMING

Information in this table assumes that you are within 2,000 feet of sea level. Review the section following this table for information about pressure canning at higher altitudes.

For **dial-gauge canners**, maintain the reading on the dial at 11 pounds of pressure. For **weighted-gauge canners**, use the 10-pound weight or setting.

Times given in the table apply to both dial-gauge and weighted-gauge pressure canners.

VEGETABLE	PINTS	QUARTS
Asparagus	30 minutes	40 minutes
Beans (green, snap, wax)	20 minutes	25 minutes
Beets	30 minutes	35 minutes
Carrots	25 minutes	30 minutes
Corn	55 minutes	85 minutes
Greens	70 minutes	90 minutes
Lima beans	40 minutes	50 minutes
Okra	25 minutes	40 minutes
Peas (shelled)	40 minutes	40 minutes
Peppers	35 minutes	n/a
Potatoes	35 minutes	40 minutes
Winter squash and pumpkins	55 minutes	90 minutes
Yams (Sweet potatoes)	65 minutes	90 minutes

Canning Low-Acid Foods

If you're canning at altitudes of more than 2,000 feet above sea level, there's no need to change the processing time for pressure canning vegetables. Instead, adjust the pressure inside the canner as follows:

Dial-Gauge Canners

ALTITUDE	PRESSURE
0 to 2,000 feet	11 pounds
2,001 to 4,000 feet	12 pounds
4,001 to 6,000 feet	13 pounds
6,001 to 8,000 feet	14 pounds

Weighted-Gauge Canners

ALTITUDE	PRESSURE
0 to 2,000 feet	10 pounds
2,001 feet and more	15 pounds

Cooking with Pressure-Canned Foods

When you're ready to prepare a meal using the produce you canned in your pressure canner, start by evaluating whether you should use the produce. Use the following guidelines to evaluate the quality of your canned goods.

Home Canning Safety Inspection

• When you take a jar of preserved vegetables out of your larder, the lid should be stuck fast to the jar and it should bow into the jar. Press down hard on the center of the lid. If it bends or pops, assume the food in the jar is not safe to eat.

• Notice whether anything sprays out of the jar when you pop the lid. Also, look for bubbles or foam in or on the canning liquid. If you observe any of these things, assume the food in the jar is bad.

• Examine the produce. Is it mushy? Slimy? Moldy? If it's any of these, assume that it's bad.

• Sniff the produce. You might not detect an off odor right from the jar, but pay attention when you heat the produce. If it has a bad odor, assume that it's bad.

If home-canned produce fails any of these examinations, do *not* taste it. Don't leave it where people or pets can eat it.

Assuming your canned goods pass your safety inspection (I've never opened a bad jar), use the produce as you would any commercially canned food products.

Assuming you've followed the prescribed canning procedures, you'll have safe vegetables that are vitamin rich and tasty.

There's Nothing You Can't Can

Mastering the fundamentals of pressure canning is very empowering. Put up a few batches of vegetables so you become comfortable with the operation of your canning pot. Then extend your expertise by cooking up mixed vegetables, soups, stews, pie fillings, and even meats and seafood to preserve in canning jars, but don't experiment! Make sure you follow recipes tested by the USDA.

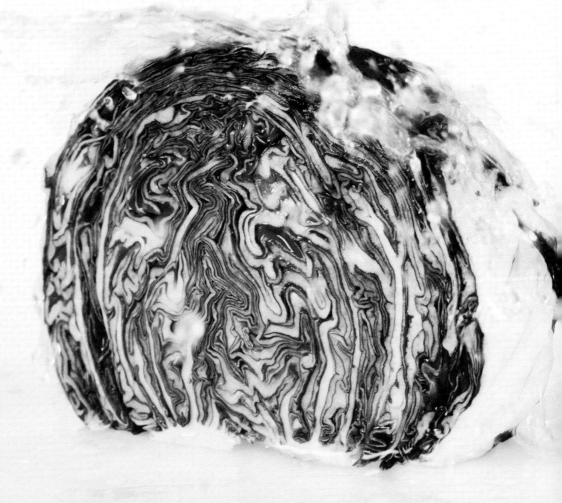

Chapter 8

Fermentation

Preserving produce isn't always about keeping it in pristine condition. Not so long ago, canning and refrigeration simply weren't available to store produce for more than a few weeks. Fortunately, our ancestors discovered that with fermentation they could control the rate at which food spoils. If they were willing to accept a gradual change in the food's flavor and texture, they could ferment and store vegetables for many months.

Today, we're so used to "clean" foods that we don't even recognize products of fermentation. When we stumble across these developing naturally in our homes, we probably throw them in the garbage. For example, cider vinegar is juice that has fermented and become bitter. Sour cream is, well, cream gone sour, while yogurt is pretty much the same thing, but usually with less fat. Wine is fermented fruit juice and beer is fermented grain "juice." Even making yeast bread involves fermentation that causes the bread to rise.

In this modern age of sterilization and clean packaging, fermented vegetables and whole fruits have all but vanished from our diets and almost no one in this country uses fermentation alone to preserve vegetables through the winter.

Fermentation

SAUERKRAUT: POSTER CHILD OF FERMENTED VEGETABLES

Most of us are familiar with two kinds of fermented vegetables:

Cucumbers and Cabbage

Cucumbers

You might ask, what fermented cucumbers? Fermented cucumbers are pickles! But let's not get too excited; most pickles we eat today are not directly products of fermentation (Chapter 9 explains how to make several types of pickles without fermenting anything).

Originally, pickles were exclusively the product of fermentation. Wooden pickle barrels held cucumbers fermenting in brine that could keep without refrigeration until every pickle had been eaten. Still, fermenting cucumbers is a terrific way to make pickles, and we'll look at pickled cucumbers a bit later in this chapter.

Cabbage

The idea of eating fermented cabbage may seem crazy until you recognize that fermented cabbage is nothing other than sauerkraut. Perhaps best known for its relationship to hotdogs, sauerkraut is available refrigerated in grocery stores throughout the United States.

To create genuine sauerkraut, you ferment cabbage under controlled conditions that let favorable bacteria thrive while preventing harmful bacteria from growing. The bacteria convert whatever sugar there is in the cabbage into lactic acid, making the cabbage sour. You can eat this fermented product raw, or cook it as a side dish or as a component of a main course.

The term **probiotic** has become a buzz word of the dieting and natural foods industries. It refers to the collection of beneficial microorganisms that live in each of us. Raw fermented vegetables are an excellent source of probiotics, so it's best not to can or freeze fermented vegetables before consuming them.

In the pure spirit of fermenting vegetables, you can store sauerkraut indefinitely in the container where you ferment it; it will taste tangier as the months wear on. The USDA, however, recommends that you freeze or can the sauerkraut for long-term storage after three to six weeks of fermentation. Either way, by fermenting them, you can extend the storage life of vegetables by months.

What Can You Ferment?

What *can't* you ferment? You needn't limit the vegetables you ferment to cucumbers and cabbage. You can ferment any vegetable you'd eat; it's as much about experimentation as it is about preserving food.

For the most consistent results, shred whatever vegetables you ferment so they're about the same thickness as cabbage leaves. This way, the sugars throughout the vegetables will break down at a constant rate. But you don't need to shred your veggies; they'll ferment all the way through even if you leave them whole.

My Roommate's Kimchi

Many years ago, I rented an apartment with a man who was wild about kimchi. I'd heard this was a popular Korean cabbage-based food typically fermented in earthen jars buried in the ground. My apartment mate fermented his in a jar in a kitchen cabinet.

I didn't pay much attention to my friend's preparations. He'd announce he was going to make kimchi and he'd take over the kitchen. He said that he liked his kimchi with a lot of garlic, and I can attest that when he opened the jar of fermenting vegetables, the aroma of garlic quickly suffused the entire apartment and, I guess, all the surrounding apartments.

I never became a fan of my apartment mate's kimchi, but fermenting vegetables today evoke strong memories of his culinary passion. Some recipes are as basic as cabbage, onions, garlic, ginger, chili peppers, salt, and water, while others include many types of vegetables and fruits together with garlic, ginger, chili powder, salt, and water. The common factor in all of these kimchi recipes is controlled fermentation.

Fermentation

Without going deep into the vegetable bins, you can create an enormous variety of fermented foods simply by adding seasonings to the old standbys of cucumbers or cabbage. Consider the variety of pickles in your grocery store: dill, sweet, bread-and-butter, garlic, half-sour, hot. With the exception of half-sours, these varieties get their distinctive flavors from the mix of sugars and seasonings in the brine. (Traditionally, a half-sour pickle was one that fermented in brine having very little salt.)

Fermented cabbage has its own traditions. Sauerkraut originated in central Europe and is an unseasoned fermented vegetable. However, kimchi, a fermented cabbage product of Korean origin, may include such flavorings as garlic, ginger, onions, and hot chili peppers, giving it a distinctive aroma and flavor.

When you ferment several types of vegetables together, the flavors mix as the sourness develops. So by combining potatoes and carrots, for example, and adding such seasonings as dill, fennel, basil, tarragon, rosemary, or sage, you can create a product that might go especially well with pork or beef or chicken or fish. Much of the fun is in mixing your own concoction, letting it ferment, and tasting it to see where it ends up.

Equipment for Fermenting Produce

Fermenting produce is not demanding on your kitchen gear. You'll need a large cutting board, an assortment of knives (a large chef's knife is very useful), a saucepan for making brine, maybe a large bowl or two, and a fermentation jar. You'll also need a plastic shopping bag and a large rubber band. Finding the right fermentation jar may be your biggest challenge.

The classic fermentation container is a stoneware crock, usually cylindrical, with impermeable glaze. These days it's much easier to find glass containers to handle the job. Don't use a metal container, as your ferment could react with it, producing unpleasant flavors or, at the least, clouding the brine.

One fermentation container I use is 9 inches in diameter, but it narrows to 7 inches at the top. A plate small enough to go into the container leaves a 1-inch ring of vegetables floating on the surface.

My favorite fermentation container is 5½ inches across, but it narrows gradually to an opening of 4 inches. I can fill this with brine up to where it begins to narrow, and use a small bowl or ramekin to weigh down vegetables that try to come to the surface.

When selecting a fermentation container, consider that you'll be using it to hold vegetables floating in liquid and that you need to keep those vegetables fully submerged in the liquid. One strategy for this is to put a plate on the vegetables with a weight on the plate. This works well when the plate is nearly the same diameter as the container.

When you read the procedures for fermenting produce, this will make more sense. So read through the steps before you acquire a fermentation container. When you have the right jar, fermenting vegetables is a snap.

How to Ferment Vegetables

Start with the freshest possible ingredients. Ideally, harvest vegetables and start them fermenting on the same day. Under the right conditions, cabbage can keep for months after harvest, so don't assume it's fresh just because you buy it at a farmers' market or farm stand.

For this example, I'm making sauerkraut, so the photographs show cabbage. Making sauerkraut is a comfortable starting point for fermenting produce, but if you want to start with other vegetables, don't be afraid; use the proportions noted here and you'll have perfectly acceptable results.

Step 1

Wash the fermentation container and the vegetables.

Step 2

Prepare the vegetables. Peel off and discard the outer leaves of cabbage heads. Cut the cabbage into strips by first cutting the head in half from top to bottom, and then slice parallel cuts starting at one edge and working across the entire half head. Cut up the heart of the cabbage as well.

Prepare Vegetables to Ferment

Shredding is the most reliable way to prepare vegetables for fermentation, but you can ferment whole vegetables, sliced vegetables, or bite-sized pieces. Shredding is especially easy with root vegetables such as carrots, beets, potatoes, turnips, parsnips, and radishes. For other vegetables, I lean toward creating bite-sized pieces as I would were I preparing them as a side dish. Wash and peel root vegetables, and then run them through the shredder disk of a food processor. Or use a vegetable peeler to cut strips from the root vegetables, or cut them into very thin sticks with a chef's knife.

Place the prepared vegetables into a large bowl (if there will be room enough in your fermentation container to toss the vegetables around with your hand, put the vegetables directly into the container); for every pound of vegetables, sprinkle 2 teaspoons pickling salt on top.

NOTE

Pickling and fermenting projects use salt to suppress the growth of unwanted bacteria, mold, and yeast. Regular table salt contains a chemical to keep it from clumping and this chemical will make the brine in a ferment cloudy. To keep the brine clear, use pickling salt or sea salt instead of table salt; neither contains an anticlumping agent. If you use sea salt, mound it in the measuring spoons a tad more, as there is slightly less sea salt in a level teaspoon than there is pickling salt—the bigger crystals in sea salt don't pack together as tightly.

Step 4

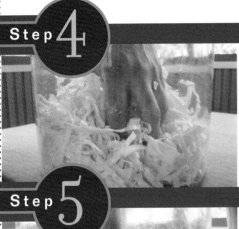

Toss the vegetables to mix in the salt completely. Don't be gentle; bruising and cracking the vegetables helps release the juices they contain.

Step 5

Pack the vegetables firmly into the bottom of the fermentation container. Again, don't be gentle. Bruise and crack the vegetables as you press them into the smallest layer you can make.

Step 6

Weigh down the vegetables. The typical strategy is to set a clean plate on the vegetables and then fill a quart-sized canning jar with water, put a lid on it, and set it on the plate.

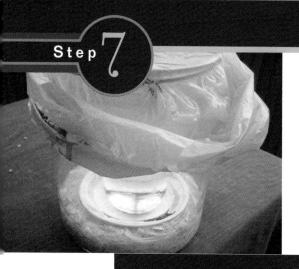

Step 7

Cover the fermentation container by pulling a plastic shopping bag over it and stretching a rubber band to hold the bag in place. Store the fermentation container in a cool, dark place.

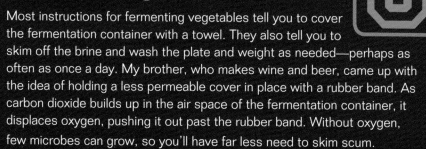

What's with the Bag?

Most instructions for fermenting vegetables tell you to cover the fermentation container with a towel. They also tell you to skim off the brine and wash the plate and weight as needed—perhaps as often as once a day. My brother, who makes wine and beer, came up with the idea of holding a less permeable cover in place with a rubber band. As carbon dioxide builds up in the air space of the fermentation container, it displaces oxygen, pushing it out past the rubber band. Without oxygen, few microbes can grow, so you'll have far less need to skim scum.

Step 8

After 24 hours, there may be enough fluid in the container to cover the vegetables. If there isn't, add brine—you need to submerge the produce. To make brine, combine 1½ tablespoons pickling salt with 1 quart boiling water. Let the brine cool to room temperature before adding it to your fermentation container. Reattach the plastic shopping bag with the rubber band.

Step 9

Monitor the fermentation. If mold forms on the surface of the brine, skim it off and wash the plate and the jar that's weighing the plate down. Then replace the plate, the weight, and the cover.

About Brine

While brine discourages unwanted microbes in fermenting vegetables, it serves another purpose as well: it limits the rate of fermentation. The beneficial bacteria that break sugar down into lactic acid work faster when the brine is less salty. If the room temperature is below 60 degrees Fahrenheit, you can speed things up by making brine with 1 tablespoon salt per quart of water.

To slow fermentation—particularly when the room temperature will be above 75 degrees Fahrenheit—make brine using 3 tablespoons pickling salt per quart of water. Vegetables will ferment even if the brine contains 5 tablespoons salt per quart of water, but they'll be practically inedible.

A brine with 1½ tablespoons salt for every quart of water produces vegetables that are noticeably salty, but not unpleasantly so.

When Fermentation Is Done

Fermented vegetables are officially sour after three or four days of fermentation; at this point, you can start eating then. However, if you're fermenting foods to extend their shelf life, you need to ferment them for a longer period. Fermentation could easily continue for four to six weeks; by this time there will be ample lactic acid in the vegetables to make them "high-acid" food. You can preserve them using a boiling water bath rather than a pressure canner.

If you prefer the less sour flavor that develops in the first week of fermentation, you'd best use freezing as your strategy for long-term storage.

Canning Fully Fermented Vegetables

Consult Chapter 5 for a description of the supplies you'll need and for step-by-step instructions for canning high-acid foods. You can hot pack or raw pack fermented vegetables.

To hot pack, place your fermented vegetables and brine in a saucepan and heat to a gentle boil. Spoon the vegetables and brine into prepared, hot canning jars. The brine should cover the vegetables and leave ½ inch of headspace.

To cold pack fermented vegetables, strain the brine into a large pot and bring to a boil as you pack the canning jars with fermented produce. Pour the boiling brine into the jars, covering the produce and leaving ¼ inch of headspace.

Whichever packing method you use, process filled and covered pint jars in boiling water for 15 minutes, and process quarts for 20 minutes. Consult the "High-Altitude Processing Times" table on page 119 for adjustments to processing time if you're not within 1,000 feet of sea level.

Fermentation

Things to Try

Even if you're not a fan of sauerkraut, you might want to ferment some vegetables. Chapter 9 explains how to make pickles without fermenting anything. However, you might enjoy fermenting cucumbers to produce pickles like the ones your grandpa's grandpa ate. Pickled peppers are pretty popular these days, and pickling via fermentation produces very distinct flavors.

If you like sauerkraut, then you're also likely to enjoy many other combinations of fermented vegetables. Take your enjoyment in new directions by creating your own kimchi. Or forget the cabbage and build a vegetable medley on a completely different flavor base. Here are some guidelines to get you started:

FERMENTED DILL PICKLES

You'll need pickling cucumbers, pickling salt, cinnamon sticks, mustard seed, peppercorns, and heads of fresh dill weed. These pickles fit the category of "half-sours."

1. Start with enough pickling cucumbers to fill your fermentation container to no more than 4 inches from the top. Wash the cucumbers.

2. You'll need about one-half to three-fourths the amount of brine as you have cucumbers by volume. For 1 gallon of cucumbers, that's 2 to 3 quarts of brine; prepare the larger amount so you know you'll have enough. To make

brine, heat water to a boil, add 2 tablespoons pickling salt for every quart of water, and let the brine cool to room temperature.

3. In the meantime, thoroughly wash your fermentation container and cut the cucumbers into the desired shape. First cut off the blossom and stem ends, and then either leave the cucumbers whole, slice them into spears lengthwise, or cut them into disks about ¼ inch thick. For dills, I cut my cucumbers into spears.

A head of dill weed is a raft of blossoms that grows on tall stalks. Harvest dill heads immediately after they bloom, if you can, but they'll impart great flavor even if you use them green.

4. For each quart of prepared cucumbers, put one-half of a cinnamon stick, 1 teaspoon mustard seed, ½ teaspoon peppercorns, and 1 head dill weed into the fermentation container.

5. Put the prepared cucumbers into the fermentation container on top of the spices and add enough brine to float the cucumbers (don't pack cucumbers down for fermentation the way you do other vegetables).

6. Follow the procedures outlined in the "How to Ferment Vegetables" section on page 204.

Sliced cucumbers may be ready in 2 weeks while spears and whole cukes may require 2 to 4 weeks to ferment. All bubbling in the brine will stop when the pickles are ready.

FERMENTED CHILI PEPPERS

Pickled peppers are popular condiments for salads and submarine sandwiches (grinders). Some folks lean toward "sweet" peppers, which are very mild, and others go for jalapeños, which range from vaguely hot to fire-alarm scalding. I particularly enjoy whole pickled jalapeños with the stems still attached: hold the stem, bite off the chili pepper, and chew your way into a sweat.

To ferment chili peppers, wash them and slice them into ⅜-inch sections. You'll produce rings with clumps of seeds suspended in their centers. Leave the seeds. If you like, add a clove of crushed garlic and a quarter of an onion for each quart of pepper slices. Put these all in your fermentation container (don't crush them down into the container as you do cabbage and other vegetables) and cover them with brine (2 tablespoons pickling salt for every quart of water); ferment according to the instructions in the "How to Ferment Vegetables" section on page 204.

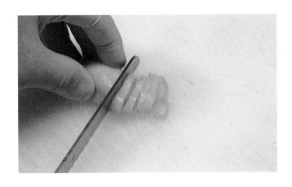

Fermentation

To ferment whole jalapeño peppers, harvest them with stems attached, wash them, and load them into your fermentation container but don't pack them down. Cover them with brine and ferment according to the instructions in the "How to Ferment Vegetables" section on page 204.

GETTING STARTED WITH KIMCHI

As I noted earlier, there is no official recipe for kimchi. In fact, I've come to think of the term kimchi as being synonymous with "fermented vegetables." When I eat kimchi, I expect very strong flavors and a little heat, and you can make kimchi with such characteristics using only a handful of ingredients. Use the same steps for fermenting vegetables but with a slight variation.

To make a relatively authentic kimchi, use Chinese cabbage (napa) rather than those round European varieties, and cut it into strips by slicing across the leaves starting at the top and working toward the root end. For each pound of cabbage strips, add 2 cloves chopped fresh garlic, 1 tablespoon grated fresh ginger, and a quarter of an onion, diced. Then mix through 2 teaspoons pickling salt for every pound of cabbage.

WARNING!

Wear gloves! Red pepper flakes will irritate any raw spots on your skin, and the oils will linger for hours, even with repeated hand washing. If you massage the chili paste into the vegetables with bare hands and later touch your eyes or lips, you could experience significant discomfort.

Before you pack this into your fermentation container, prepare some chili paste and massage it through the prepared, salted vegetables. To make chili paste, for each pound of cabbage mix 1 teaspoon dried red pepper flakes, 2 teaspoons sugar, 1 teaspoon sesame seeds, and a few drops of juice to make a paste (lemon, lime, apple, orange—you can even use water). Be thorough when you mix this with the vegetables; try to get some on every piece of cabbage.

Now pack the vegetables into your fermentation container and complete the process as described in the "How to Ferment Vegetables" section, starting with Step 5 on page 205.

PORK AND SAUERKRAUT?
HAPPY NEW YEAR!

When I moved to central Pennsylvania, I had never heard mention of "pork and sauerkraut." Once here, I learned that pork and sauerkraut is a traditional party food eaten to kick off the new year. It's a Pennsylvania Dutch tradition reflecting the belief that you'll have a great year if your first meal is pork and sauerkraut.

You can probably guess that there are many ways to prepare this traditional meal. This may be one of the easiest, but the results are very satisfying. There are two ingredients:

> Boneless pork loin
>
> Sauerkraut

Buy enough pork to serve ¼ pound to each diner. Estimate the volume of the pork and have two to three times as much sauerkraut on hand (if it looks like 1 quart of pork, you need 3 quarts of sauerkraut). Finally, you need a covered casserole dish large enough to hold the pork loin with 1 inch or more of clearance on all sides, and 2 or more inches of clearance on top.

Line the bottom of the casserole dish with about 1 inch of sauerkraut and add enough brine to match the depth of the fermented cabbage. Lay the pork loin fat side up on the sauerkraut and brine, then pack more sauer-kraut along the sides and ends of the pork until it's covered by at least 1 inch of sauerkraut. When the casserole dish is packed properly, it should appear to be a dish full of kraut—you shouldn't be able to see the pork loin.

From the Tip Jar

If you don't have a covered casserole dish to handle this job, use a large roasting pan and a roasting bag. Pack the pork and sauerkraut into the bag so that the pork is completely surrounded by sauerkraut, close the bag tightly, and cut one or two slits in the top of the bag.

Cover the casserole dish and place it in a 200 to 225 degrees Fahrenheit oven for 8 to 12 hours. Check the casserole from time to time and if it seems dry, add water (adding more brine can make the pork very salty).

When you peel back the sauerkraut, the pork should be tender and moist; it will fall apart when you place a fork in it and pull gently. To serve, prepare a bed of the cooked sauerkraut on a plate and lay several chunks of pork in the middle.

Fermentation

FERMENTED FRUITS

In more than forty years, I've not heard anyone mention home-fermented fruit, yet this delicacy has enthusiastic advocates. I learned about fermented fruit when my family lived in Italy and a friend gave my mom a small container of what we called "mother."

Mother was like sourdough starter, but it was fruit based rather than flour based. You could keep a small portion of mother in a container at room temperature for months. To benefit from it, you'd add fruit, which after a few days of fermentation, developed a tangy alcoholic bite. My mom served this fermented fruit as a dessert topping or as a dessert that stood on its own.

Mom smuggled her fermented fruit mother into the United States way back when and kept it alive for many years. It must have stopped working (added fruit rotted rather than fermented) at some point, and my mom had no idea how to restart it. That's the last I heard about home-fermented fruit.

Your Own Starter

Plenty of people are familiar with fermented fruit, and it's easy to start your own. The methods for doing this vary, depending on who you ask, but they all have something in common: they all call for yeast you'd use to bake bread.

Instructions for making fermented fruit can be daunting. Some tell you to check on the starter daily and add fruit and sugar every two weeks. I'm more of a set-it-and-forget-it person, so I suggest you make a starter that requires little oversight.

The only special equipment you need to ferment fruit is a nonreactive fermentation container. Choose either a glazed crock or a glass jar with a loose-fitting cover. Depending on your sense of aesthetics, you might opt to use a plastic shopping bag held on by a rubber band to cover your fermentation container, but a screw-on lid not fully tightened makes an adequate cover. This container should have at least a 2-quart capacity.

From the Tip Jar

Friends and family may be enthusiastic about fruit fermentation. Share the fun with them when your fermentation container is full by measuring 1½ cups of fruit and syrup into a clean container that they can take home and use as starter.

Here's how to make and handle fermented fruit starter:

1. Thoroughly clean your fermentation container.

2. Combine 1 cup warm (but not hot) water with 1 cup sugar and 1 tablespoon active dry yeast. Stir until the sugar dissolves.

3. Pour the mixture into a fermentation container (or you can just prepare the mixture directly in the container), cover the container, and set it aside for 3 or 4 days at room temperature.

4. On that third or fourth day, cut up fruit into bite-sized pieces, preparing 3 level cups. Among my favorite fruits are peaches, pears, cherries, grapes, and pineapple, but use what you have available.

Preparing Fruits to Ferment

The classic fermented fruit mix seems to consist of peaches, pineapple, and cherries. Never fear, you can ferment any fruit, though some work out better than others and a few may disappoint you.

For example, bananas and strawberries may not hold up as well as other fruits, and blackberries a nd raspberries may over-whelm the ferment with their own strong flavors. One way to manage strong-flavored fruits is to use a smaller proportion of them relative to other fruits. You'll have to de-cide whether the consistencies or flavors of various fermented fruits appeal to you.

Apples and Pears

Wash, peel, core, and then cut them into bite-sized pieces. Apples tend to change color when you process them (think apple cider), so they aren't a great choice for fermentation.

Stone Fruits

Peaches, apricots, nectarines, and plums all ferment well. Wash, skin, and pit them, and cut them into bite-sized pieces.

Berries

Wash berries and remove stems or caps. Cut large berries (specifically, strawberries) in half.

Cherries

Use sweet or sour cherries. Wash, stem, and pit them before adding them to the ferment.

Citrus Fruits

Oranges, limes, lemons, and grapefruit contain a lot of acid, which will slow fermentation. Introduce only small amounts of any of these fruits. To prepare them, wash the fruits, cut them in half, and dig out the segments with an appropriate-sized spoon or a sharp knife. Remove the seeds.

Grapes

Wash grapes and cut them in half. If the grapes contain seeds you don't need to remove them, but doing so creates a more appealing dining experience later on.

Melon

Wash them and remove the rind and seeds. Cut the melon into bite-sized chunks.

Pineapple

While quite acidic, pineapple is a great addition to fermented fruit. Prepare it by washing it, cutting off the rind, and then cutting the softer part of the fruit into bite-sized chunks.

5. Add 3 cups sugar to the liquid in the fermentation container and stir for several minutes to encourage the sugar to dissolve.

6. Add the prepared fruit and stir to mix thoroughly.

7. Cover the container with a loose-fitting lid and store it in a dark place at room temperature. Wait at least 2 weeks before consuming any of the fermenting fruit.

There's no hurry to use fermented fruit; it will be fine if you leave it alone for several months. When you do want to eat some, spoon out as much as you'd like as long as you leave at least 1½ cups of fruit and syrup in the jar.

Serve fermented fruit on its own or spoon it over ice cream, sponge cake, pound cake, pudding, or yogurt. You can refresh the container anytime by adding equal amounts of fruit and sugar. So if one day you (and a friend) chow down 2 cups of fermented fruit, replace it by adding back about 1½ cups of fruit and 1½ cups of sugar—but expect to wait another 2 weeks before the fermentation matures.

THE ALCHEMY OF FOOD PRESERVATION

Mixing up brine and vegetables starts a process that recalls ancient civilizations. So many cultures have employed fermentation to preserve vegetables and fruit and to produce drinks that would keep for months or even years. Participating in this storied history is quite a rush.

The first time I fished a pickled cucumber from a fermentation container and bit into it, I was truly astonished at its fresh flavor and crisp texture. It was as if I'd turned lead into gold. Now I usually have at least one batch of vegetables fermenting throughout the growing season. I hope you'll ferment some produce and enjoy it as much as I do.

From the Tip Jar

If it seems as though the "mother" isn't effective at fermenting additional fruit, mix 1 teaspoon baker's yeast with 1 tablespoon warm water, then stir this mixture into the fruit and syrup mixture. Give it a few weeks to work its magic.

Quick Pickling

Acidic Brine = Flavor + Storage

Quick pickling is about submerging food in liquid that contains a balance of sugar, salt, and acid designed to stymie enzymes that make food rot and to keep microorganisms from growing. In extreme cases, brine alone can preserve food for a very long time. However, it's far more common to put the food and the brine in canning jars and process it in a boiling water bath canner to kill microbes and seal out air that might cause spoilage.

Through quick pickling, you can make just about any variety of pickled cucumber, a huge assortment of relishes, pickled vegetables such as beets and peppers, and even pickled fruits such as pears, peaches, and cherries. Stored at room temperature, these pickles will last for a year or longer.

If fermentation is about controlling the speed at which foods spoil, quick pickling is about submerging food in mature pickling brine so fermentation never takes place. Quick pickling achieves the same goal as fermentation without the wait.

Quick Pickling

Equipment for Quick Pickling

For basic pickles, quick pickling involves packing canning jars with produce, covering them with brine, and processing in boiling water. Making relish is a bit more involved, requiring time chopping and mixing vegetables (and sometimes fruit), cooking the mixture, and then canning the finished product.

So the equipment you need for quick pickling is pretty much what you use for canning high-acid foods. In fact, to succeed with quick pickling, read Chapter 5 before you try any of the projects in this chapter. I'm assuming you understand canning, and I'll refer to Chapter 5 for canning-specific procedures.

Along with the canning equipment, you'll need some big nonreactive containers such as stainless steel, glass, or ceramic bowls, pots, or canisters.

More than any other method of preserving food, quick pickling is about recipes. To preserve produce as pickles, you need to mix an appropriate brine and assemble the proper seasonings. If your brine doesn't provide the correct balance of acid, salt, and sugar, dangerous microorganisms could grow in your pickles or relish.

Salt in Your Quick Pickles

Virtually every quick pickle recipe I've seen calls for salt, some, quite a bit. In pickling through fermentation, salt suppresses the growth of unwanted bacteria, but beneficial bacteria don't mind it so much. Over time, those beneficial bacteria break down sugar, producing carbon dioxide and lactic acid.

Vegetables that ferment in salt brine eventually stabilize when the acid becomes strong enough to kill—or at least to debilitate—the beneficial bacteria.

With quick pickling, you immediately submerge produce in very acidic brine. Then, except in the case of refrigerator pickles, the heat of canning combines with the acid to kill or debilitate just about any microbes in the food.

So why all the salt in quick pickle brines? Flavor! Without salt, your quick pickles won't taste much like their naturally fermented counterparts.

Always start with tested recipes when you preserve foods by quick pickling. If you change the recipes, it's okay to increase the amount of vinegar in proportion to the amount of water, but never decrease the proportion of vinegar to water. If the pickles are too sour, increase the amount of sugar. Feel free to increase the salt in your brine. But once there's more than about 2 tablespoons per quart of liquid, there's too much salt for me.

Seasoning Pickles

You can use any combination of spices to flavor pickles, but the same small list of seasonings appears in recipe after recipe for quick pickling. This list includes onions, turmeric, mustard seed, and celery seed.

Start with this universal base, then add other seasonings to create unique flavors. A single crushed clove of garlic added to each pint canning jar of pickles, for example, will infuse the product with a distinct garlic flavor. You might try adding ¼ teaspoon shaved fresh ginger to each pint, or ¼ teaspoon dried red pepper flakes (more if you like to sweat when you eat pickles).

Other common quick pickling seasonings include cinnamon sticks, dried peppercorns, coriander, dill seed (or dill heads), allspice, and bay leaves. You can buy products labeled as "pickling

spice" in most grocery stores, and each brand is likely to include at least some of the seasonings from this list.

When pickled, the flavor of fruit may not stand up well against the vinegar in the brine. Throw in some heavy seasonings and you might lose the fruit flavor completely. Seasonings such as tarragon, cinnamon, ginger, nutmeg, and mint can complement fruit, and substituting honey for some of the sugar can provide an exotic kick.

Start with one of the basic quick pickling recipes, and vary the spices to suit your tastes.

When you make large batches of pickles, don't mix the seasonings in with the brine. That makes it almost impossible to distribute equal portions of seasonings into the canning jars. Rather, put a measured amount of spices in the bottom of each canning jar. Then add the vegetables and pour in hot brine to fill the jars.

Quick Pickling

Before you get started, a word about vinegar: these pickling recipes assume that the vinegar you use is at least 5 percent acid. If you haven't done any quick pickling, there's no reason you'd know this, but commercially bottled vinegar notes its acid content on the label. Chances are you already buy vinegar that's 5 percent acid, but it's important to check before you start pickling with it.

Refrigerator Pickles

The only characteristic that defines refrigerator pickles is that you store them in your refrigerator. Some recipes lead to very sour refrigerator pickles and others lead to sweet pickles. Because you don't can these pickles, they're more about having something pickle-y to eat than they are about preserving food.

Here are the seven steps for making refrigerator pickles that lean toward sweet:

Makes 4 to 5 cups

²/₃ cup white or cider vinegar (5 percent acid)

1 cup sugar

½ teaspoon turmeric

½ teaspoon mustard seed

½ teaspoon celery seed

1 teaspoon pickling or sea salt

1 quart cucumbers (5 four- to five-inch cukes)

1 medium-sized onion

1. Heat the storage jar (or jars) by running them through the dishwasher or boiling them in a pot on the stove.

2. Cook the vinegar and sugar in a saucepan until the sugar dissolves. Remove the pot from the heat and stir in the turmeric, mustard seed, celery seed, and salt.

3. While the brine cools, wash the cucumbers and slice them into 1/16- to ⅛-inch-thick disks.

4. Peel the onion and cut it into thin rings. Toss the onion rings together with the sliced cucumbers in a glass or stainless steel mixing bowl.

5. Pour the seasoned brine over the cucumbers and onions and toss the mixture until you've coated everything.

6. Pack the cucumber and brine mixture into one or more glass containers. Press the vegetables firmly into the jar and add enough brine to cover them. Cover the jar, rinse the sides and bottom (if you didn't spill brine down the sides of the jar, your heart just wasn't in it), and store the jar in your refrigerator.

7. Wait at least 24 hours before you sample the pickles, then eat them at your own pace; they'll improve in flavor over the first 3 or 4 days, and they'll keep for at least 1 month in the refrigerator.

See? No canning involved!

BREAD-AND-BUTTER PICKLES

Honestly, bread-and-butter pickles and refrigerator pickles are nearly interchangeable. In my experience, bread-and-butter pickles are a bit more sour. Of course, you cook bread-and-butter pickles. Some recipes call for cooking the cucumbers in brine for a hot pack into canning jars. Other recipes have you raw pack the cucumbers and add hot brine. In both cases, process the jars in boiling water long enough to cook the cucumbers completely.

CRISP PICKLES

Strategies for making crisp pickles abound, and they are reasonably interchangeable. Actually, you can use more than one strategy in a single batch of pickles and increase your chances that every bit of your preserved vegetables will produce a pleasing crunch.

Cold Curing

A common technique in quick pickling recipes, cold curing involves lowering the temperature of cucumbers and other vegetables below the freezing point of water. To do this, you typically cut the vegetables into the shapes you wish to can— spears, disks, slivers—and then submerge them in salt water with lots of ice in it.

The temperature of the salty ice water can drop as low as 28 degrees Fahrenheit, and you hold the cucumbers in it for three hours so they too become very cold. Then you immediately pack the vegetables in jars, add the pickling brine, and process in a boiling water bath canner.

Pickling Lime

For a few dollars, you can buy pickling lime from most stores that sell canning equipment. Pickling lime contributes calcium to the vegetables, which somehow works with naturally occurring pectin to make the vegetables crispier.

You mix pickling lime with water, and then float the prepared cucumbers and other vegetables in it for three or more hours. Then you pour off the water and rinse the cucumbers thoroughly at least three times to remove as much of the lime as you can. If you fail to rinse the vegetables well, the lime will interact with the acid in the pickling brine and the brine might not preserve the pickles adequately.

Alum

You can easily find quick pickling recipes that call for alum. Again, you use alum in water to soak vegetables before putting them in brine and canning them. Alum, however, is toxic in large amounts and is a bit touchy to work with (it's not fun if you inhale it, for example). So, given the alternatives available, I suggest you use different ways to crisp your pickles. Cold curing and liming are both effective, and you might also have some luck with grape leaves.

Grape Leaves

If they are available, grape leaves can play a part in your pickle-crisping strategy. For each pint of pickles you pack, put one well-washed grape leaf in the jar. Chemicals in the leaf will help keep the pickles crisp as they cook and cure in the pickling brine.

Since you're heating up the canning pot to can any pickles anyway, here's a recipe that should fill eight or nine pint jars with bread-and-butter pickles, enough to fill your canning pot. Compare this with the recipe for refrigerator pickles, and you'll see the difference is mostly about quantity and canning.

Bread-and-Butter Pickles

Makes 8 pints

4 quarts cucumbers (about 20 four- to five-inch cukes)

4 medium-sized onions (or 2 large onions)

5 tablespoons pickling or sea salt

5 or more pounds of ice

5 cups white or cider vinegar (5 percent acid)

5 cups sugar

2 teaspoons turmeric (divided)

2 teaspoons mustard seed (divided)

2 teaspoons celery seed (divided)

1. Rinse the cucumbers using a vegetable brush to remove soil, if necessary. Cut the cucumbers into the shapes you wish the pickles to have. Bread-and-butter pickles are typically ⅛- to ¼-inch disks, so cut slices across the cucumbers, discarding the end pieces.

2. Peel the onions and cut them into ½-inch wedges. Separate the layers and put them together with the cucumbers into a large bowl, pot, or plastic bucket that you'd be willing to eat out of. Ideally, use a container that can hold more than double the quantity of cucumbers and onions.

3. Sprinkle the salt through the vegetables, mixing it in with your hands until you've distributed it thoroughly. Then cover the vegetables with water and dump the ice on top. If the vegetables float to the surface of the ice water, put a plate on the vegetables and set a weight such as a canning jar full of water on the plate. Let the vegetables steep for 3 hours.

Pick Picklers, Please

Some cucumbers are better for pickling than others. Such varieties may have a version of the word pickling in their names. For example, there are cucumbers called 'Boston Pickling Improved', 'Picklebush', 'National Pickling', 'Parisian Pickling', and 'Rhinish Pickle'. When selecting seeds to grow your own pickling cucumbers, you'll find that most commercial seed packages clearly identify appropriate varieties.

If you're buying cucumbers for pickling, establish whether there is wax on the skins. In storage and shipping, wax helps hold in moisture and you really don't notice it in a salad or when you eat cucumbers raw. Unfortunately, waxed pickling cucumbers don't absorb acid and flavorings consistently. Especially when you pickle them whole, you'll get very unsatisfactory results.

So if the merchant tells you there's wax on the cukes, don't buy them for pickling. And if the merchant doesn't know whether there's wax, don't chance it; buy your pickling cucumbers elsewhere.

4. During the third hour that your cucumbers are steeping, prepare your canning pot, eight pint canning jars, lids, and bands according to the instructions in "Basic Steps for Boiling Water Bath Canning" (page 112) in Chapter 5. If you use quart jars, you'll need only four of them.

NOTE

When you cold cure cucumbers for quick pickling in this recipe, you don't need to add salt to the pickling brine. Some of the salt you add to the cold water bath sticks to the cucumbers when you transfer them to the canning jars or hot pickling brine. This is enough to provide saltiness in the finished pickles.

5. In a large stainless steel cooking pot, combine the vinegar and sugar and heat to boiling, stirring occasionally to help the sugar dissolve.

6. While the vinegar and sugar heat, pour the salt water and ice off the cucumbers and onions. Drain the vegetables thoroughly.

7. When the vinegar and sugar mixture starts to boil, add the vegetables all at once, being careful not to splash the hot brine on yourself. Stir the cucumbers into the brine and continue stirring until the brine just starts to boil. Then immediately remove the pot from the heat.

8. Fill the hot canning jars with the vegetables and hot brine. To fill a pint jar, first place ¼ teaspoon each of turmeric, mustard seed, and celery seed into it. Then pack the cucumbers and onions tightly inside and ladle the hot brine in to cover the vegetables. Leave ½ inch of headspace in the jar. To fill a quart jar, double the amount of spices specified for pints.

9. To put the lids and bands on the jars, follow the instructions in "Basic Steps for Boiling Water Bath Canning" (page 112) in Chapter 5. Process pints for 10 minutes and quarts for 15 minutes, adjusting for altitude according to the "High-Altitude Processing Times" table (page 119) in Chapter 5.

These pickles are ready to eat as soon as the jars cool, and they'll continue to improve with time. Store the jars in a cool, dark place and they'll keep for a year or longer.

Quick Pickling

Dill Pickles

Dill pickles are typically quite sour compared to bread-and-butter pickles. You make them with no added sugar. There's enough salt in this recipe to match what people traditionally refer to as "half-sours," and the lack of sugar lets the acid dominate. The main seasoning is dill weed. As with the bread-and-butter pickles, you'll cold cure these before canning. After that, these quick pickles are remarkably simple.

Makes 8 quarts

7 quarts cucumbers (35 four-
to five-inch cukes)

10 or more pounds of ice

4 1/4 cups white vinegar (5 percent acid)

8 3/4 cups water

6 tablespoons plus 1 1/2 teaspoons pickling salt

7 cloves garlic

7 dill weed branches

7 heads of dill

7 jalapeño peppers

1. Rinse the cucumbers using a vegetable brush to remove soil, if necessary. Cut the bud and stem ends off and discard them, then slice the cucumbers lengthwise into quarters.

2. Place the sliced cucumbers into a large container, add enough water to cover them, and dump the ice on top. If the cucumbers float to the surface of the ice water, put a plate on the cucumbers and set a weight such as a canning jar full of water on the plate. Let the cucumbers steep for 3 hours.

3. During the third hour that your cucumbers are steeping, prepare your canning pot, seven quart canning jars, lids, and bands according to the instructions in "Basic Steps for Boiling Water Bath Canning" (page 112) in Chapter 5.

4. In a large stainless steel cooking pot, combine the vinegar, water, and salt and heat to boiling, stirring occasionally to help the salt dissolve.

5. While the brine heats, pour the ice and water off the cucumbers and drain thoroughly.

6. When the brine reaches a boil, lower the heat to hold the boil and then fill the hot canning jars. To fill a quart jar, crush a clove of garlic and drop it into the jar. Then add one dill branch and one dill head. Cut lengthwise slits on opposite sides of a jalapeño pepper, and add it to the jar. Without crushing them, pack in as many cucumbers as will fit. Make sure no cucumber is higher than 1/2 inch below the top of the jar. Finally, pour the boiling brine into the jar to cover the cucumbers, but leave 1/2 inch of headspace.

7. To put the lids and bands on the jars, follow the instructions in "Basic Steps for Boiling Water Bath Canning" (page 112) in Chapter 5. Process quarts for 15 minutes, adjusting for altitude according to the "High-Altitude Processing Times" (page 119) table in Chapter 5.

Store the canned pickles in a cool, dark place and let them rest for 4 weeks or longer before opening them.

No Cucumbers Required

All this discussion has been about pickling cucumbers, but please don't let that narrow your focus. I've had great results from quick pickling mixed vegetables in a brine that was one part white vinegar to every two parts water, and that contained 2 tablespoons pickling salt for every quart of brine.

I use mixed pickled vegetables in cooking: I make sweet-and-sour pork several times a year, and the dish gets its "sour" from pickled vegetables. Here's how to pickle mixed vegetables like mine:

1. Prepare your canning pot, seven quart canning jars, lids, and bands according to the instructions in "Basic Steps for Boiling Water Bath Canning" (page 112) in Chapter 5.

2. While the canning jars come to a boil, prepare your vegetables. I use an assortment of carrots, broccoli, cauliflower, bell peppers, and onions. Wash the vegetables. Peel the carrots and cut them into bite-sized disks. Cut up the broccoli and cauliflower into bite-sized pieces. Cut up the peppers, discarding the seeds, and peel and slice the onions into quarters, separating the layers.

Do not prepare all of a particular vegetable at once. Alternate your preparations among the various vegetables so you have about the same amount of each at any point. Stop preparing vegetables when you have enough to fill as many jars as you want to process.

Quick Pickling

3. Mix the vinegar, water, and salt in a saucepan and bring to a boil. For 7 quarts of vegetables, you'll need about 5½ quarts of brine. That would require 7⅓ cups vinegar, 14⅔ cups water, and 11 tablespoons salt.

4. Pack the hot jars. To fill a quart jar, select an even distribution of vegetables and pack them into the jar as tightly as possible without crushing them. Shake the jar as you fill it to encourage the vegetables to settle. Finally, fill the jar with the boiling brine, leaving ½ inch of headspace.

5. To put the lids and bands on the jars, follow the instructions in "Basic Steps for Boiling Water Bath Canning" (page 112) in Chapter 5. Process quarts for 20 minutes, adjusting for altitude according to the "High-Altitude Processing Times" table (page 119) in Chapter 5.

These pickled vegetables aren't about eating right out of the jar. Please try them in my recipe for sweet-and-sour pork.

Sweet-and-Sour Pork

I make no claims for the Chinese-ness of my sweet-and-sour pork. I learned to make it when I was in high school, and when I cook this dish now, I pretty much guess on proportions. The dish gets its "sweet" from the light syrup of canned pineapple, and its "sour" from the brine of canned pickled vegetables. Sometimes there's not enough sweetness in the pineapple juice so I add a little sugar to the wok to balance the pickle juice. Making sweet-and-sour pork is very much a "mix-and-taste" operation in my kitchen. Serve this sweet-and-sour pork dish with cooked white rice.

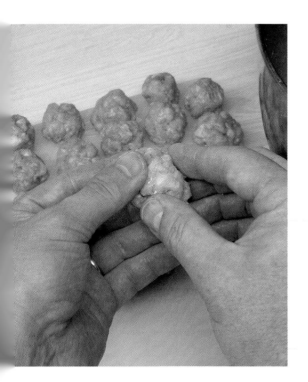

Makes 4 servings

1 ¼ pounds ground pork

¼ cup bread or cracker crumbs

1 egg

3 tablespoons soy sauce (divided)

1 teaspoon grated fresh gingerroot (divided)

½ to 1 cup vegetable oil (divided)

1 clove garlic, smashed and

   finely chopped (optional)

1 fresh onion, cut into bite-sized pieces

1 quart pickled vegetables

3 tablespoons sherry or cooking wine

1 teaspoon sesame oil (optional)

1 pint canned pineapple chunks

1 cup chicken stock

2 tablespoons cornstarch

1. In a large bowl, combine the pork, bread crumbs, egg, 1 tablespoon of the soy sauce, and ½ teaspoon of the grated ginger. Work the ingredients together thoroughly. Then shape the mixture into ½- to ¾-inch balls.

Rolling each meatball in cornstarch makes the meatballs easier to handle.

NOTE

2. Pour enough vegetable oil into a medium-sized frying pan to fill it at least ½ inch deep. Place the pan on medium-high heat and when the oil is hot, cook the meatballs in batches. Carefully set the meatballs in the oil with at least ½ inch between them. Cook the meatballs until the bottoms are brown, then roll them over, cooking for a total of 2 to 3 minutes per side. Remove them from the oil and let them drain on a plate lined with paper towels.

I prefer to cook the pork balls in a frying pan rather than a wok because the frying pan lets me easily maintain the spacing between them. In a wok, meatballs tend to roll together in the middle.

3. Heat about 3 tablespoons vegetable oil in a wok or large frying pan on high heat and tilt the pan to coat the sides and bottom. Add the garlic, the remaining ½ teaspoon grated ginger, and the onion and stir to keep things from burning.

4. Drain the pickled vegetables, saving the brine, and add the vegetables to the wok. Cook the vegetables while stirring until they heat through and begin to singe just a bit.

5. Add the remaining 2 tablespoons soy sauce, the sherry, and the sesame oil, if using, to the wok, lower the heat to medium, and put a lid on it. Let the vegetables cook for 3 to 5 minutes.

6. While the vegetables cook, open the jar of pineapple and pour the juice into a measuring cup. However much pineapple juice you measure, measure half that amount of the reserved pickle brine. Add both the pineapple juice and the pickle brine to the wok, raise the cooking temperature back to high, and stir to mix the juices through the vegetables.

7. When the liquid in the wok is bubbling, add the pineapple chunks and the meatballs. Continue to toss the ingredients until the liquid begins to boil again, then add the chicken stock. Mix everything together and taste the liquid in the wok! If it's sour, add 1 tablespoon sugar. If it's sweet, add 1 tablespoon pickle brine. Make it taste right to you.

8. Put ¼ cup water or chicken stock in a measuring cup or small bowl, add the cornstarch, and mix thoroughly. Pour about half of the mixture into the wok and stir. The liquid in the wok should thicken; you're looking for the thickness of a hearty stew, so add more of the cornstarch mixture and stir if the sauce looks thin.

Quick Pickling

Relish!

Pickle relish is omnipresent at burger restaurants and it may be the best-known condiment after mayonnaise, ketchup, and mustard. But if pickle relish is your only exposure to the world of relishes, you're in for a treat: home canning lets you preserve many types of produce in relish form.

Vegetables alone require pressure canning as they contain very little acid. However, by combining acidic vinegar and sugar with chopped or ground vegetables, you create delicious new flavors and turn the vegetables into high-acid foods that can just fine in a boiling water bath.

With thousands of relish recipes available, I encourage you to surf the Internet and ask friends for recipes to try. Making relish may involve a lot of prep work, but it's usually quite easy to do well. To get you started, I've included my two favorite relish recipes. One is chili sauce my mom used to make, and the other is pepper relish that my mother-in-law served at dinner parties.

Mom's Chili Sauce

I want to make it clear that my mother didn't invent this relish. I'd like to give credit to its creator, but my recipe card reads simply "Charlotte's Chili Sauce," and any information about its source died with my mother years ago.

The resulting sauce (see page 234) is chunky, wet, sour, and sweet. Mom usually spread a generous amount on top of meatloaf before baking it. To my taste buds, this boosted the meatloaf from a family meal to gourmet fare. I still use this sauce on meatloaf, and any generic meatloaf recipe will do.

How to Peel a Tomato (or Peach or Apricot)

The ideal tomato for canning is perfectly ripe. Such a tomato gives up its skin quite easily if you slit it with a sharp knife, pinch the edge of the skin between your thumb and the knife blade, and gently peel the skin away (below). However, when you're peeling twelve, twenty-four, or one hundred tomatoes, do yourself a favor and cook the skins off them.

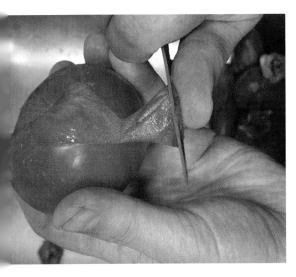

If the skins haven't cracked, gently slip the tip of a knife through the skin to get things started. When you pinch the skin between your thumb and the knife blade and pull, the skin will almost slide off the tomato (below).

This technique works as well with peaches and apricots.

To do this, find a pot that will hold five or six (or more) tomatoes at once. Fill it with water and bring the water to a boil. Float five or six tomatoes in the water for 45 to 60 seconds, fish them out with a strainer, and plunge them into cold water.

Quick Pickling

Mom's Chili Sauce

I have a second favorite use for Mom's Chili Sauce: I use a few tablespoons in a three-egg omelet along with a generous amount of cheese. I'm embarrassed to admit that my favorite "cheese" for this is classic or low-fat Velveeta (no, really, I like good-tasting food too).

Makes 2 to 3 pints

2 green peppers

2 medium-sized onions

12 large tomatoes, peeled

1 cup white or cider vinegar (5 percent acid)

1¼ cups sugar

1 tablespoon salt (table salt will do)

½ teaspoon ground cloves

2½ teaspoons ground cinnamon

1. Stem and seed the peppers, peel the onions, and chop the tomatoes, onions, and peppers into ⅛-inch pieces. I use a knife to chop the vegetables so I don't risk reducing them to meal; this chili sauce should be chunky.

2. Put the chopped vegetables into a medium-sized saucepan along with all the remaining ingredients. Mix well and bring the vegetables to a boil. Then lower the heat and simmer uncovered for 3 hours.

3. In the last hour of cooking, prepare your canning pot, jars, lids, and bands according to the instructions in "Basic Steps for Boiling Water Bath Canning" (page 112) in Chapter 5. Ladle the cooked chili sauce into pint jars and process them for 15 minutes, adjusting for altitude according to the "High-Altitude Processing Times" table (page 119) in Chapter 5.

Mom-in-Law's Red Pepper Relish

Come to dinner at my house several times and you might conclude that where hors d'oeuvres are involved, we lack imagination. In truth, we don't often have hors d'oeuvres, so when we do, we prefer to have only the very best. My mother-in-law's red pepper relish delivers.

To serve this amazing hors d'oeuvre, place an 8-ounce block of cream cheese or Neufchâtel cheese on a serving platter about an hour before your guests arrive. Empty a 4-ounce container of red pepper relish onto the cheese, spreading it to the edges of the block. Then distribute crackers on the platter around the cheese and relish. Use Ritz, Club, Triscuit, or water crackers, whichever you prefer. When your guests arrive, place a butter knife or two on the serving platter. To eat, cut off a chunk of cheese along with the relish that sits on top of it. Smear that on a cracker, and chow down. Here's how to make the red pepper relish:

Makes enough to fill about 10 four-ounce jars

12 large red peppers

1 tablespoon salt

2 cups cider vinegar (5 percent acid)

3 cups sugar

1. Core, seed, and chop the peppers into the consistency of fine meal. I've done this with a food processor and with a meat grinder (my mother-in-law's suggestion). The job is much easier when you use a meat grinder.

2. Stir the salt through the chopped peppers and let it stand for 2 hours. Then transfer the mash to a strainer and let it drain for about 1 hour. Capture all the liquid and use it to make Three-Bean Red Pepper Dressing as directed on page 236.

3. Combine the peppers, vinegar, and sugar in a saucepan, stir well, and simmer for 3 hours. Stir the relish several times an hour for the first 2 hours, and increase the frequency of stirring especially during the last 30 minutes.

Red pepper relish becomes thick and dark as it cooks. This batch is ready for canning in a boiling water bath.

4. During the last 30 minutes of cooking, prepare your canning pot, canning jars, lids, and bands according to the instructions in "Basic Steps for Boiling Water Bath Canning" (page 112) in Chapter 5. Spoon the relish into 4-ounce jars and process them for 15 minutes, adjusting for altitude according to the "High-Altitude Processing Times" table (page 119) in Chapter 5.

Three-Bean Red Pepper Dressing

When you make red pepper relish, you can collect a lot of salty pepper juice. I always hated throwing the stuff out, so I came up with a great way to use it. This is a little hit-or-miss because you can't be sure how much juice you'll collect. I've put together a table to help you make a good mix:

Pepper Juice	Vinegar	Sugar
1 cup	1/3 cup	1/2 cup
1 1/2 cups	1/2 cup	3/4 cup
2 cups	2/3 cup	1 cup
2 1/2 cups	2/3 cup + 3 tablespoons	1 1/4 cups

Prepare several 4-ounce canning jars, lids, and bands for boiling water bath canning according to the instructions in "Basic Steps for Boiling Water Bath Canning" (page 112) in Chapter 5.

In a saucepan combine the pepper juice you've collected with the corresponding amount of vinegar and sugar from the preceding table. Optionally, add 1 teaspoon fruit pectin per cup of pepper juice. Bring this syrup to a boil. Load the hot syrup into the hot jars, leaving 1/2 inch of headspace, and process for 15 minutes in a boiling water bath canner, adjusting for altitude according to the "High-Altitude Processing Times" table (page 119) in Chapter 5.

Three-Bean Salad

This classic picnic food gets a small twist from red pepper dressing. Plan for it, of course, by canning your own green and wax beans. Substitute fresh-cooked beans when they're in season.

Makes 6 to 8 servings

1 pint canned green beans

1 pint canned wax beans

1 (15 ounce) can black, kidney, or pinto beans

1 small onion, finely chopped

1 (4-ounce) jar canned Three-Bean Red Pepper Dressing (see preceding directions)

⅓ cup olive oil

Ground black pepper to taste

Drain the beans and combine them in a large bowl with the remaining ingredients, tossing to coat the beans. Set the bowl in the refrigerator for 4 or more hours. Mix the salad once or twice during the refrigeration to coat the beans with the dressing, and mix it once more just before you serve it.

Quick Pickling for Fame and Glory

Most people don't can. Close to half of those who do report making quick pickles as their first canning projects. Apparently, pickles are popular.

Your knowledge of quick pickling puts you in a rarified position: as you discover more delicious recipes for pickles and relishes, you'll have more unique gifts to offer your canning-challenged friends and family. There's nowhere else they'll find the goodies you can produce in your own kitchen.

I hope you'll keep exploring and experimenting, and that you'll share your enthusiasm for preserving food so that more people will discover the benefits and joys of these simple techniques.

Bibliography

I consulted many authorities as I wrote this book. Most important, I reviewed publications from the United States Department of Agriculture (USDA) whose research and guidelines represent the greatest body of information on food-storage safety. Cooperative Extension offices all over the United States offer USDA publications intended for enthusiasts of home canning, freezing, and other preservation techniques. Please contact the office nearest you.

Armstrong, Eric. "Ultimate Kimchi." *TreeLight.* 2004. Web. Spring 2010. <http://www.treelight.com/health/nutrition/UltimateKimchi.html>.

"The Best Ever Bread and Butter Pickles." *Squidoo: Welcome to Squidoo.* 2010. Web. June-July 2010. <http://www.squidoo.com/bread-and-butter-pickles->.

"Candied Orange Peels." *Inspired Bites.* 6 August 2008. Web. Spring 2010. <http://inspiredbites.blogspot.com/2008/08/candied-orange-peels.html>.

CM. "Fresh Refrigerator Pickles." *Cooks.com - Recipe - Fresh Refrigerator Pickles.* Web. Spring 2010. <http://www.cooks.com/rec/view/0,1736,134184-255199,00.html>.

Complete Guide to Home Canning. Bulletin #539 ed. [Washington, D.C.]: U.S. Dept. of Agriculture, Extension Service, 2006. Print.

"Crisp Dill Pickles." *Cooks.com - Recipe - Crisp Dill Pickles.* Web. June-July 2010. <http://www.cooks.com/rec/view/0,1736,158182-247203,00.html>.

De Long, Eric. "Storage Guidelines for Fruits & Vegetables." *Gardening Cornell -* Storage.pdf. Web. Spring 2010. <http://www.gardening.cornell.edu/factsheets/vegetables/storage.pdf>.

De Sandoval, Lynette. "Fermented Fruit—Care and Feeding." *Timotheus' & Lynnette's Brewing Page.* 2006. Web. Spring 2010. <http://brewing housezacharia.com/LogNotesL/FFcare.html>.

East, Mae. "Bread And Butter Pickles Recipe - Food.com - 71203." Food.com - *Thousands Of Free Recipes From Home Chefs With Recipe Ratings, Reviews And Tips.* 12 September 2003. Web. Spring 2010. <http://www.food.com/recipe/bread-and-butter-pickles-71203>.

"Expected Vegetable Garden Yields - Vegetables | Lawn & Garden | LSU AgCenter." *The Louisiana State University Agricultural Center | LSU AgCenter - To Innovate, Educate, and Improve Lives Through Research and Education.* 28 August 2007. Web. Spring 2010. <http://www. lsuagcenter.com /en/lawn_garden/home_gardening vegetables/Expected Vegetable Garden Yields.htm>.

Gist, Sylvia. "Successful Cold Storage." *Backwoods Home Magazine.* July-August. 2003:
35. Web. Spring 2010. <http://www.backwoodshome.com/articles2/gist82.html>.

"Heirloom Cucumber Seeds - Huge Selection of Open Pollinated Cucumber Varieties."
*Heirloom Seeds - Over 1300 Varieties of Non-hybrid Seeds including Heirloom
Vegetable Seeds, Heirloom Flower Seeds and Heirloom Herb Seeds.* Web.
June-July 2010. <http://www.heirloomseeds.com/cucumbers.htm>.

Howard, Sharon. "Dill Pickles Recipe - Allrecipes.com." *AllRecipes.com - the Top
Web Site for Recipes, Food and Cooking Tips.* 2003. Web. June-July 2010.
<http://allrecipes.com//Recipe/dill-pickles/Detail.aspx>.

Katz, Sandor Ellix. "Vegetable Fermentation Further Simplified." *The Revolution Will Not
Be Microwaved: inside America's Underground Food Movements.* White River
Junction, VT: Chelsea Green Pub., 2006. Wild Fermentation. Web. Spring 2010.
<http://www.wildfermentation.com/resources.php?page=vegetables>.

Kim, Ben. "Traditional Korean Kim Chi Recipe." *Natural Health: Chet Day's Huge Collection
of Healthy Eating Recipes and Natural Health Articles.* Web. Spring 2010.
<http://chetday.com/kimchirecipe.htm>.

Lent, Max. "Max's Fresh Refrigerator Pickles." *InfoRochester.com Pickle1.* 2010. Web. Spring
2010. <http://www.inforochester.com/pickle1.htm>.

"Making Fermented Pickles and Sauerkraut." *University of Minnesota Extension.* 2009. Web.
May-June 2010. <http://www.extension.umn.edu/distribution/nutrition/dj1091.html>.

Nazlina. "Alum for Pickling - Safety Guideline How to Use This Chemical." *Pickles and
Spices World - Experience a Unique Outlook from a Malaysian Cook.* Web.
June-July 2010. <http://www.pickles-and-spices.com/alum-for-pickling.html>.

"RecipeSource: Friendship Fruit Starter." *RecipeSource: Your Source for Recipes on
the Internet.* Web. Spring 2010. <http://www.recipesource.
com/fgv/fruits/friendship-fruit-starter01.html>.

Rodriguez, Barbara. "Making Fermented Pickles." *Organic Gardening - Home Page.* 2009. Web.
Spring 2010. <http://www.organicgardening.com/feature/0,7518,s1-5-83-793,00.html>.

Tong, Cindy. "Harvesting and Storing Home Garden Vegetables." *University of Minnesota Extension.* Web. Spring 2010. <http://www.extension.umn.edu/distribution/ horticulture/DG1424.html>.

United States of America. Department of Agriculture. Michigan State University Cooperative Extension. *Yields of Michigan Vegetable Crops.* By Bernard H. Zanstra and Hugh C. Price. E-1565 (Revised) ed. E. Lansing: Michigan State University, 1988. Destiny Farm. Web. Spring 2010. <http://www.destinyfarmgardens.com/Yields_20of 20commercial_20vegetable_20crops_20MSU_1_.pdf>.

————Department of Agriculture. National Center for Home Food Preservation. *University of Georgia.* Web. Spring 2010. <http://www.uga.edu/nchfp/>.

————Washington State University. Clark County Extension. *Food Safety & Nutrition: Fruit Pickles* by Sandra Brown. Web. Spring 2010. <http://clark.wsu.edu/family/ specific-foods/FruitPickles.pdf>.

"Vintage Fruit Starter." *Cooks.com - Recipe - Vintage Fruit Starter.* Web. Spring 2010. <http://www.cooks.com/rec/view/0,1719,147172-249196,00.html>.

Yu, Jennifer. "Candied Orange Peels Recipe." *Use Real Butter.* 9 October. 2007. Web. Spring 2010. <http://userealbutter.com/2007/10/09/candied-orange-peels-recipe/>.

Zwirn, Lisa. "Pickled Fruit Adds Flavorful Touch to Dishes." *The Boston Globe. Boston.com.* 17 September. 2008. Web. Spring 2010. <http://www.boston.com/lifestyle/ food/articles/2008/09/17/pickled_fruit_adds_flavorful_touch_to_dishes/>.

Index

Yes, I Did!

Canning Notes

Date

Yes, I Did!

Canning Notes

Date

Yes, I Did!

Canning Notes

Date

_____

_____

_____

_____

_____

_____

_____

_____

_____

_____

_____

_____

_____

_____

_____

_____

_____

_____

_____

_____

_____

_____

_____

Yes, I Did!

Canning Notes

Date

_____

_____

_____

_____

_____

_____

_____

_____

_____

_____

_____

_____

_____

_____

_____

_____

_____

_____

_____

_____

_____

_____

_____

A book for any gardener, anywhere.

Click onto the

garden BOOKSTORE.net

Every Gardening Book in Print

Meet Daniel Gasteiger

Daniel Gasteiger is a hayseed turned city slicker turned city slipper. As a kid he raised horses and vegetables at his parents' weekend farm. After college, Daniel moved to Boston, Massachusetts, where he worked in the emerging personal computer industry. As Daniel and his wife, Stacy, started a family, they moved back to the country where they live on about a third of an acre on the edge of a small town.

Daniel grows a small kitchen garden from which he squeezes an enormous amount of produce. He blogs about gardening and preserving food on several websites, and posts videos on YouTube that share stories and techniques from his garden and kitchen. He lives with his wife and children in Lewisburg, Pennsylvania. This is his first book with Cool Springs Press.

Daniel invites you to visit and participate. You'll find him at:

http://www.smallkitchengarden.net
http://www.homekitchengarden.com
http://www.fooddryer.net